RESEARCH HIGHLIGHTS IN SOCIAL WORK 18

Privatisation

Other titles in the Research Highlights in Social Work series

Social Work Departments as Organisations
Edited by Joyce Lishman
ISBN 1 85302 008 7

Working with Children
Edited by Joyce Lishman
ISBN 1 85302 007 9

Evaluation: 2nd Edition
Edited by Joyce Lishman
ISBN 1 85302 006 0

Why Day Care?
Edited by Gordon Horobin.
ISBN 1 85302 049 4

Sex, Gender and Care Work
Edited by Gordon Horobin
ISBN 1 85302 001 X

**Living with Mental Handicap: Transitions in the Lives of
People with Mental Handicap**
Edited by Gordon Horobin and David May
ISBN 1 85302 004 4

Child Care: Monitoring Practice
Edited by Isobel Freeman and Stuart Montgomery
ISBN 1 85302 005 2

Sex, Gender and Care Work
Edited by Rex Taylor and Jill Ford
ISBN 1 85302 016 8

Performance Review in Social Work Agencies
John Tibbitt and David Pia
ISBN 1 85302 017 6

Social Work and Disability
Edited by Mike Oliver
ISBN 1 85302 042 7

Social Work Response to Poverty and Deprivation
Edited by Ralph Davidson and Angus Erskine
ISBN 1 85302 043 5

RESEARCH HIGHLIGHTS IN SOCIAL WORK 18

Privatisation

Jessica Kingsley Publishers
London

Editor: Richard Parry
Secretary: Anne Forbes
Editorial Advisory Committee:

Professor G. Rochford	University of Aberdeen
Professor J. Cheetham	University of Stirling
Dr J. Lishman	Robert Gordon's Institute of Technology
Mr S. Montgomery	Strathclyde Region Social Work Department
Mr D. Murray	Tayside Region Social Work Department (SSRG Scotland)
Dr A. Robertson	University of Edinburgh
Dr P. Seed	University of Aberdeen
Mr J. Tibbitt	Social Work Services Group, Scottish Office

University of Aberdeen
Department of Social Work
King's College
Aberdeen

First published in Great Britain in 1990 by
Jessica Kingsley Publishers Ltd
118 Pentonville Road
London N1 9JN

British Library Cataloguing in Publication Data
Privatisation - (Research highlights in social work; 18).
 1. Great Britain. Public welfare services
 I. Parry, Richard II. Series
 361.6'0941

 ISBN 1-85302-015-X
 ISSN 0955-7970

Printed in Great Britain by
Billing & Sons Ltd, Worcester

CONTENTS

The Contributors

Richard Parry

Richard Parry is a Lecturer in Social Policy in the University of Edinburgh. Formerly he worked for the Department of the Environment and the Centre for the Study of Public Policy at the University of Strathclyde. He is the author of the United Kingdom sections of the multi- volume study *Growth to Limits: the Western European Welfare States since World War II* (edited by Peter Flora, de Gruyter 1986-7) and the Social Policy Chapter of *Developments in British Politics 2* (Macmillan 1986). He is also the author of *Scottish Political Facts* (T & T Clark 1988) and co-editor of *The Scottish Government Yearbook*.

Paul Wilding

Paul Wilding has been Professor of Social Policy at the University of Manchester since 1981. He is co-author (with Vic George) of *Motherless Families* (1972), *Ideology and Social Welfare* (2nd ed. 1985), and *The Impact of Social Policy* (1984), all published by Routledge and Kegan Paul. He has also written *Professional Power and Social Welfare* (RKP 1982) and edited *In Defence of Welfare* (MUP 1986).

Gerald Wistow
Melanie Henwood

Gerald Wistow is Senior Lecturer in Health and Social Care Management at the Nuffield Institute, University of Leeds. He has a long-standing interest in community care and relationships between health, local government and non-statutory agencies. He has published widely on such issues and is the co-author of six books. His current interests include: managing the mixed economy of care; developing the user dimension; and the organisation of night nursing services. Melanie Harwood joined the King's Fund Institute as a Health

Policy Analyst in June 1989. Between 1983 and 1989 she was a Research Officer with the Family Policy Studies Centre, working especially in the area of community care for frail elderly people. She was previously engaged in research at the University of Bath into policy and service co-ordination.

Linda Challis

Linda Challis is a Lecturer in Social Policy at the Centre for the Analysis of Social Policy at the University of Bath. She has worked in the Personal Social Services in both a practice and research capacity. Her present research interests are in the care of elderly people and the relationship between public and private provision. She has been a member of national working parties on aspects of care for both children under five and elderly people, as well as serving as a member of a District Health Authority.

Robin Darton
Ken Wright

Robin Darton is Research Fellow in the Personal Social Services Research Unit at the University of Kent at Canterbury, and has been part of the PSSRU team commissioned to monitor and evaluate the Care in the Community Initiative, from which the book *Care in the Community: the First Steps* has been published. A statistician, with research interests in health and social services provision for elderly people, he has been involved in two major surveys of residential and nursing homes, the latest in collaboration with Ken Wright, Senior Research Fellow and Deputy Director of the Centre for Health Economics at the University of York. Ken Wright's main research interests are in the economics of long-term care, especially the transition to community care. Although the main emphasis in his research projects is on the micro-economic evaluation of alternative forms of care for people with chronic disabilities, he is also involved in a further major survey on the residential care of people with a mental handicap in collaboration with Dr Norma Raynes at the University of Manchester.

Judith Phillips
Peter McCoy

Judith Phillips is a Research Associate with the Social Work Development Unit at the University of East Anglia. After studying at Aberystwyth, Stockholm and Oxford, she worked as a field, residential and community social worker. She is currently completing a PhD on the process of admission to private residential care for elderly people. Peter McCoy is Principal Planning Officer with Suffolk Social Services, and previously worked for the London Boroughs of Southwark and Bexley doing social services research. His main interests are social gerontology and computer based learning.

Ernie Lightman
Christa Freiler
John Gandy

Ernie Lightman is Professor of Social Policy at the University of Toronto, Faculty of Social Work. Christa Freiler is Program Director with the Metropolitan Toronto Social Planning Council. John Gandy is Professor Emeritus at the University of Toronto Faculty of Social Work.

Stephen Shaw

Stephen Shaw is Director of the Prison Reform Trust. He worked formerly in the Home Office Research Unit and for the National Association for the Care and Resettlement of Offenders. He has written extensively on both economic and criminal justice issues.

The Private Challenge for Practitioners

Richard Parry

If a spectre has stalked British social policy in the 1980s, it is that of privatisation. After many years in which the principal task seemed to be the perfection of the public sector as an accountable and efficient provider of services, the question now is whether any area of policy can remain immune to the pressure of private sector activity. Practitioners must come to terms with practical as well as philosophical questions about the matter, and the relationship between these two aspects is the focus of this book.

In a sense privatisation is a meaningless concept. The private sector has always existed in most areas of welfare provision; where it is small and weak, this is because market forces have made the public sector the best answer for clients and customers. The individual and the state are often able to choose whether the public or the private sector provides the best instrument to achieve objectives. Theorists of the 'mixed economy of welfare' have emphasised that public provision need not be synonymous with public financing, but have not necessarily demonstrated how the right balance between the two is to be achieved.[1]

In the 1980s the context of this public/private choice has altered. The Conservative government uses privatisation as a means to reduce the market power of public employees and to give more scope to private entrepreneurs. Local authorities have had to accept competitive tendering and the use of outside contractors, hemmed in as they are by legislation on the one side and the auditor on the other. Practitioners cannot dismiss the private sector as a minimal influence on their job. Clients respond to the insecurity of public supply by diverting their rising discretionary income into welfare services.

This book highlights some of the challenges posed by privatisation to those who have to make social welfare services work. The centrepiece of the book presents some recent research in the service where private supply has increased most rapidly - residential care, especially for the elderly. Linda Challis reviews recent policy developments; Robin Darton and Ken Wright discuss the findings of a major survey into the characteristics of homes; Judith Phillips and Peter McCoy report their research into practitioners' attitudes. These are preceded by introductory chapters on the privatisation issue (Paul Wilding) and on the impact of private growth on social services planning (Gerald Wistow and Melanie Henwood). The final chapters widen the horizon into North America (Ernie Lightman, John Gandy and Christa Freiler) and private prisons (Stephen Shaw).

The extent of private provision

There are wide variations in the extent of private sector provision in social policy (see table 1). Education and health have relatively small private sectors, increasing in the 1980s but still far from being a substitute for public provision. Housing has become predominantly private, with those dependent on public services socially marginalised; a similar pattern is evident in transport. But two services - pensions and residential care for the elderly - have a public-private balance; about half of the client group is supplied by the private sector. Residential accommodation for the mentally ill, mentally handicapped and physically disabled under sixty five also has a large private and voluntary sector component - respectively forty two, thirty six and sixty six per cent in 1986 (*Social Trends*, 1988 edition, tables 7.29 and 7.30). In these cases there is a public-private symbiosis. The public sector underwrites the private through fiscal and social security policy, and becomes a provider-of-last-resort. It is here that Conservative policy is liable to move from the mere facilitation of private supply to its positive promotion on favourable terms.

Table 1: Private sector shares of activity			
	1979	1983	1987
Housing (% dwellings)	67	70	72
Pensions (% workforce covered)	50	52	n/a
Elderly residential (% places)	33	39	48
Health (% population insured)	5	8	9
Education (% school pupils)	5.5	6.0	6.6

Sources: Pensions *Employment Gazette*, December 1985, 434-437; housing *Housing and Construction Statistics*, 1977-87, table 9.3; remainder *Social Trends*, 1989 and previous editions.

In social policy as a whole, the private sector cannot compete with the 'market dominance' of the public sector. For all sorts of reasons connected with the avoidance of 'poor risks' it would not even seek to. But it can use the right to private supply guaranteed in most areas of the welfare state to seize commercial opportunities in fields where people may wish to apply their income and savings to social care. Residential provision for the elderly is the clearest example of this: it combines a fairly modest capital investment (certainly by comparison with a school or hospital) and a supply of finance from both public and private sources. A similar pattern is found to a lesser extent in residential care of the mentally ill and mentally handicapped.

The reasons for privatisation

Most practitioners and observers in social policy take an explanatory attitude to the issue similar to the critical stance taken by Paul Wilding in the opening chapter of the book. This attitude is formed partly by a political commitment to egalitarian causes, but it also reflects practical knowledge of the circumstances of service delivery. In contrast, much New Right thinking (such as that expounded by Patrick Minford[2] and Digby Anderson[3]) derives from either political theory or economics and is divorced from what used to be called 'social administration' - a body of theory grounded in the practical experience of care agencies.

Throughout the 1980s the public sector has had to give ground both practically and intellectually. Disquiet about 'monolithic public sector bureaucracies' has become a commonplace of democratic socialist thinking, as in the Labour Party's policy review of 1989. Service delivery agencies of government - social services, education and health authorities - have lost their room for manoeuvre, and been forced to differentiate their activities into discrete operations whose performance can be tested against market alternatives. This builds upon an irony of the public sector: that those activities which yield a marketable product may be tested and found wanting, whereas those which produce an undifferentiated public good like security or advice to politicians may be protected. Public sector contraction has moved from the nationalised industries through the manual activities of local government to professional services. Concepts of permanence and security in public employment, of the job as something 'owned' through tenure, are being replaced by a *de facto* contractual basis in which the reward is specific to the task performed.

But above all the impetus for privatisation has come from the preoccupation with the efficient use of public money. Many social policy professionals rightly highlight the weakness of the crude minimisation of the cost of inputs. The difficulty with this criticism is that the trend of the 1980s is to move from qualitative to quantitative indicators of performance. In practice this means testing established practices against possibly cheaper alternatives. Attempts in the 1970s to establish a secure methodology for cost-benefit or cost-effectiveness analysis were unsuccessful, and in the process the notion of a comprehensive value of a public service was lost. It has been replaced by a demand to declare immediate cost savings which is astonishingly unsophisticated when set against the initial objectives of public expenditure planning in Britain.

It is easy to identify the weakness of a public policy that pays out £1bn a year of social security money to the elderly in residential accommodation, or neglects the cost of redundancy in awarding a service contract to a private firm. But privatisation is the expression of a particular political and economic framework. It represents a departure from the rationality and social concern found in many practitioners, and does not seek justification against the norms of professional training in health and social work. Rather it asserts the primacy of risk and uncertainty in the management of public business, with the public sector seen as an instrument of a minimal set of tasks rather than as the expression of a social order to be set against the capitalist basis of the economy.

Why has the old notion of the public sector as the setter of standards of care and of model employment practices had so many critics? One reason is the weakness of 'labourist' thinking - socialist in provenance but corporatist in practice because of the influence accorded to professionals and trades unions. This approach is vulnerable to accusations that services are being run in producers' rather than consumers' interests. Also important is a preoccupation with tight financial targets, especially during a financial year. This requires a flexibility in the management of resources much easier to achieve in a private sector environment of rapid adjustment of supply to changes in market demand. More generally there is a disappointment with the achievement of many post-war Labour governments at both central and local level, a matter of excessive expectations and inattention to performance and to the standards of service actually received by the consumer.

The North American example

Perhaps the best way of understanding Conservative policy is as the Americanisation of social protection. The American pattern is of minimal provision, except in old age; wide variations in the level of benefits; the social segregation of welfare into class-specific institutions; and the widespread use of 'third sector' suppliers through contracts and purchase-of-service. The differentiated welfare states[4] these produce are much less secure against changes of economic and political circumstances.

As Lightman et al. show in their chapter, even a system as welfare-orientated as Canada's can fall prey to privatisation. In Canada's case, this takes the form of a Minister for Privatisation at federal level, and pressures in many of the provinces for a greater use of purchase of private and voluntary service. Even after decades of public welfare provision, the suspicion that only private supply can guarantee efficient and appropriate provision is very strong. This is compounded by a move from voluntary to commercial supply with a neglect of evidence about standards of care.

The positive aspects of privatisation

If privatisation is redefined as freedom from state control of practice, there are positive aspects. The hospice movement, alternative education, rehabilitation, list D schools, intermediate treatment and holistic medicine all rely on being at arm's length from professional orthodoxy. They cannot do so comfortably within the same structure as the standard public provision. A network of successful projects, relying on grants and fees for service, may well be the preferable system if the objective is to encourage innovation and client choice.

With organisational independence comes therapeutic freedom. Many professionals value above all else the chance to work intensively with clients of their choice and without interference. This applies particularly to the group treatment of children with behavioural difficulties, the adult mentally handicapped, and the confused elderly. Statutory services are often happy to place and finance their clients with owner/practitioners whose credentials are proven. Such 'caring entrepreneurs' enrich the private sector and serve as examples of good practice.

The organisation of health in Britain has shown that the limitation of the model of the independent professional lies in the fact that it still requires predominant public financing but cannot ensure public control. The disputes about the contracts of consultants and general practitioners show the dangers of distancing practitioners from direct public employment. They become no less dependent on public funds, but their activities are more difficult to monitor and their notion of professional freedom expresses itself in resistance to change. It is only a minority of gifted practitioners which is truly able to benefit from the freedom to mix public and private work.

In fact, the social work profession may have a greater claim than the medical to the benefits of independent status. Many parts of social care have a quasi-judicial aspect, expressed in the office of *guardian ad litem* (which can be held on a self-employed basis), and in the need for proper management of the financial interests of dependent clients. A plurality of provision requires dispassionate advice to clients, which may not easily be given by an employee of a providing agency (the problem explored in Judith Phillips' and Peter McCoy's chapter). The recent growth of the freelance social worker[5] may be part of a new trend.

The 'savings' of privatisation

Improvement in service or reduction in cost cannot be conjured out of thin air by the private sector; and yet the whole case for privatisation rests upon the evidence of improvements in cost or efficiency. The variables involved require careful and non-rhetorical analysis, something they rarely receive. They reflect some combination of:

a) more efficient input (such as the use of less experienced staff for any given input; involvement by managers and proprietors; and failure to train staff or to release them for training and management development);

b) non-sharing of overheads such as central administration, research and personnel management, with a ratchet effect operating if a public sector agency contracts and the central capability must be spread across a narrower range of operating units;

c) different care management - the extent of cover and supervision, and physical aspects such as the number of single rooms.

Evidence from a number of studies, especially by PSSRU, shows that the private sector's circumstances enable it to deliver apparent savings of 15-25 per cent.[6] This matches the saving obtainable by competitive tendering exercises, even when the winning tender comes from the in-house workforce.[7] Conservative contentions have been substantiated by this evidence of a margin for improvement, and yet the concept has to be heavily qualified by the existence of non-attributed costs - paying off the present workforce, subsequent loss of competitiveness, and a possible loss of service to clients. The 'success' of privatisation depends upon some crude notions of cost and efficiency appropriate to the debating chamber but not the research institute. Nor is the evidence all one way. Gibbs and Smith have shown that many private nursing homes seem capable of improving their quality by ten to thirty per cent, given their charges.[8]

The caricatures - of private sector as yielding efficiency, or public sector as protecting care - are equally wrong. Rather we must think seriously about what we want from services and whether they need to be in a particular sector. Fundamentally, the public sector regulates and underwrites the whole system, and sometimes a 'clean slate' will be necessary in order to tilt the balance from producers to consumers. Sometimes this can only happen by quitting the public sector, especially in times of contraction which inhibit investment and changes in working practices.

There are two more serious questions. The first is the lack of a level playing-field on cost savings, because the privatising authority has to bear the cost of liquidating its own operation. When redundancy is taken into account the first-year costs at least tend to be unfavourable. The issue is just how extraordinary the non-recurrent costs are.

The second is that the full balance sheet on the costs of private provision is not known in the short-term. Typically, defects in quality of provision come to light through scandals (deaths or media reports). Inquiries into these tend to reveal a history of bad practice, often associated with poor physical conditions and poor supervision of staff. This is not a purely private sector phenomenon: it could be argued that the long chains of command in the public sector are less well able to detect problems. The real difficulty is that the political timescale for privatisation is very short in comparison with the care process. The public sector may have liquidated itself before it knows what it is doing.

The limits of privatisation

It has long been thought unthinkable that the core functions of the state's jurisdictional framework - police, justice, prisons, tax collection - should be privatised. As long-standing public functions, they should in theory show the virtues of full public control and accountability; there are any number of discouraging pre-modern examples of private sector involvement. But most objections miss the point. They suggest, rightly, that the state cannot abandon responsibility for these areas and that coercive powers should be exercised by the state alone. But the technical provision of services need not be a state monopoly. Service standards are a matter of proper procedures, which are not guaranteed by the provision of services by the state. Contractual arrangements in which standards are specified and can be monitored may be a better way of improving public service.

In fact security is one function where we may have been mistaken in analysing the boundary between public and private goods. The flourishing market in private security guards, and the frustrations felt by the government in managing British prisons, are part of the same problem of public sector inadequacy. Public expenditure constraints are a major problem, but even if unlimited resources were available the social and political trends to privatise seem to be strong. A public/private mix as a tool for managers and customers to use against producers is becoming the pattern even here, as Stephen Shaw notes in his chapter.

Conclusion

The lesson from the papers in this book is that practitioners cannot stand aside from the public/private issue. They must enter into an exchange relationship with a private sector that will surely become a more prominent part of total provision. This will involve the transfer of clients between sectors; the purchase of private or voluntary service on grounds of cost as well as care need; and the introduction of a financial and managerial framework in statutory services akin to the private sector. More precisely, the upward drift in costs implicit in being both a good employer and a provider of a normatively high standard of care will have to be questioned.

This raises the question of the political and social values held by practitioners. Many have been taken by surprise as the values of enterprise and privatisation have been extended during the 1980s. But, as in other spheres of British society, we should not assume that the norms of the 1960s and 1970s are set for all time. There are earlier traditions which still have resilience, especially among Conservatives. In the field of social provision, they include a paternalistic and potentially stigmatising attitude to clients; a parsimony in the application of public funds; a wish that public provision should be overtly non-extravagant and unpretentious; a 'public service' ethic distrustful of trade union rights for employees; and a preference for voluntary action as the means of setting the agenda of public concern. The notion of social citizenship has become the intellectual orthodoxy of practitioners, but it has never taken deep enough root to displace the older traditions in the public mind.

A vision of the future may be seen in Labour-controlled local authorities which have been successful in adapting to the circumstances of the 1980s. For instance, Strathclyde Regional Council commissioned research from the Institute of Local Government Studies at Birmingham University and in 1989 is seeking to implement its recommendation for a more consumer-responsive service. Under the threat of contracting-out imposed by the Local Government Act 1988, direct service organisations have started to outdo their private competitors in managerial firmness when negotiating new contracts. A combination of indifference to trades unions and solicitude to consumers turns on its head the approach of the 1960s and 1970s.

Privatisation is a sea-change which has happened because the public sector has failed to win sufficiently the confidence of the electors who sustain it through their taxes. However disreputable the arguments employed or misguided the people who believe them, the political reality of privatisation has affected all political parties. But the intellectual reality of the arguments in favour of public provision remain no less potent - provided they can be realised in practice.

References

1. For a summary, see Knapp, Martin. 'The Mixed Economy of Welfare: a Stop-gap Solution' *Public Money*. September 1986.

2. Minford, Patrick. 'The Role of the Social Services: the View from the New Right'. In Loney, Martin (Ed.) *The State or the Market*. Sage, London, 1987.

3. Anderson, Digby, Lait, June and Marsland, David. *Breaking the Spell of the Welfare State*. The Social Affairs Unit, London, 1981.

4. Mishra, Ramesh. *The Welfare State in Crisis*. Wheatsheaf, Brighton, 1984.

5. See 'Inside the Independent Sector' *Community Care*. 26 November 1987.

6. Judge, Ken. 'Value for Money in the British Residential Care Industry'. In Culyer, A.J. and Jonsson (Eds.) *Public and Private Health Services*. Blackwell, Oxford, 1986.

7. Domberger, Simon, Meadowcroft, Shirley and Thompson, David. 'The Impact of Competitive Tendering on the Costs of Hospital Domestic Services' *Fiscal Studies*. 8, 4, November 1987, 39-54.

8. Gibbs, Ian and Smith, Peter. 'Private Nursing Homes: Providing Good Value?' *Public Money and Management*. Spring 1989, 57.

Privatisation: an Introduction and a Critique

Paul Wilding

'Privatisation' is the contribution of the Thatcher governments to the vocabulary of politics. Prior to 1979 the word scarcely appeared in political debate. The theme hardly featured in the 1979 Conservative Manifesto but since 1982 privatisation has become a central element in Government policy.

In some ways it is odd that it did not emerge sooner. It expresses the beliefs of the government about the superiority of market forces and about the necessity of rolling back the state. It expresses, too, more specific dissatisfactions about the role and performance of public enterprises and the effectiveness, efficiency and cost of the social services. For a government committed to tax cuts, privatisation offers revenue raising as an alternative to cuts in expenditure.

For market economists, privatisation is a means to an end: greater competition leading to greater efficiency. For the present government privatisation has tended to become an end in itself, the product of the belief that ownership is the key variable in economic performance.

Though the Thatcher government has been enthusiastic about privatising public enterprises it has been much more circumspect in its approach to the privatisation of welfare. And yet privatising welfare is quite central to the achievement of New Right goals. Welfare state employment accounted for nearly sixty per cent of government employment by the late 1970s and it is the welfare functions of government which make up the largest part of government spending.[1] A government concerned to cut public sector employment and reduce public expenditure must either impose cuts in these areas or privatise them - or better still both. But the British people like their social services more than they like their public enterprises. Hence the government's problem.

After two terms the government had, apart from its sale of council houses, done little more than nibble at the welfare cake. In the third term it looks as though the government's confidence may have grown but there is no definite sign yet of major moves such as education vouchers or compulsory private health insurance rather than a tax funded NHS. What we are considering is a policy in embryo.

What is privatisation?

'"Privatisation"', Donnison writes, 'is a word invented by politicians and disseminated by political journalists. It is designed not to clarify analysis but as a symbol, intended by advocates and opponents of the processes it describes to dramatise a conflict and mobilise support for their own side. Thus it is a word which should be heavily escorted by inverted commas as a reminder that its meaning is at best uncertain and often tendentious'.[2]

There is, however, a core element which appears in all the various manifestations of privatisation - the desire to strengthen and expand the market at the expense of the state and increase the exposure of the public sector to market forces. Privatisation is therefore about the denationalisation and liberalisation of public enterprise. It is about aid to the private sector as a deliberate policy to attract it to certain fields of work.[3] In relation to welfare state policies, privatisation is about reductions in state provision, reductions in state subsidy and reductions in regulation.

Reductions in state provision can, of course, be achieved in various ways. The state can simply end its involvement in the provision of a particular service - for example free dental inspection or eye checks. It can reduce the public role by a policy of cuts and reductions in services, thus forcing would-be clients to make provision privately. The state can also reduce public provision by selling off public goods - for example local authority houses.

Reductions in state subsidy can mean that individuals have to pay a larger share in the cost of a service. The reduction of rent subsidies for local authority tenants moves council housing away from a public service and towards a market orientation. Increases in prescription charges since 1979 have aimed to reduce the subsidy going to the relatively small proportion of the population who pay prescription charges.

Privatisation is also about reducing the regulatory role of the state. Since 1979 the control of private sector rents has been reduced - the aim being to return private rented housing to the market. The Fair Wages Resolution which aimed to ensure minimum wages for certain groups of workers was rescinded in September 1983, reducing the state's regulatory role in the determination of wages.

It is actually, of course, much more complicated than this. There can be reductions in the state provision of welfare alongside a continuation of public financing. There can be increases in public expenditure to finance private provision - for example in residential care for the elderly. Alternatively, a service can continue to be produced publicly while its financing is privatised. We still have a dental service which is part of the NHS but it is increasingly financed from charges levied on patients.

'Privatisation may be said to take place', Walker writes, 'when responsibility for a service or a particular aspect of service passes, wholly or in part, to the private sector and when market criteria such as profit or ability to pay are used to ration or distribute benefits and services'.[4] The argument needs, however, to be made a little more explicit. Privatisation is not just the transfer of the production or financing of welfare to the private sector. It is also about the transfer of the production and financing of welfare from the state to individuals and families and the voluntary sector. The present government's stress on the glories of family care and the 'informal sector' is a thick strand in its privatisation policy.[5]

Privatisation is therefore an approach rather than a policy. It can appear in a range of different policies.

Aims, beliefs, assumptions

The government's privatisation policy is driven by a range of beliefs and assumptions. Private and voluntary provision of welfare is regarded as normal and natural because, through most of history, that has been the mode, and because welfare services are seen as not intrinsically different from other market goods. Mrs Thatcher and her ministers have gone out of their way to stress the centrality - and even the primacy - of the contribution of the non-statutory sector. The government argument would be that the chimera of state welfare has driven out and suppressed other forms of welfare provision. The government's aim is to re-create a genuinely mixed economy of welfare with the private sector restored to its rightful place as equal - or even senior - partner.

Privatisation represents a clear attack on the welfare responsibilities which the state has assumed since 1948 and the idea of the role of the state in welfare which undergirds these responsibilities. Public provision and/or public responsibility are seen as unnecessary and inferior to other supply mechanisms. Privatisation taps a groundswell of concern about the efficiency and effectiveness of state welfare, the implications for the economy of large scale public provision - 'the public burden model of welfare' - and its supposed anachronistic nature in a society with rising real incomes.

Privatisation as a clear and determined policy is new, but the meeting of the need for welfare by private and voluntary provision is not. The significance of the aims of the privatisation policy are that it seeks to challenge what have come to be accepted beliefs about the proper spheres of the public and private sectors.

The aims, beliefs and assumptions embedded in the government's privatisation policy can be analysed under three headings - economic, political and social.

Economic

Since 1979 a central concern of government policy (and a central failure) has been to reduce public expenditure so that taxation can be cut and the productive energies of the nation released. Expansion in welfare state employment, services and transfer payments have been the major factors in the growth of public expenditure in all western countries since 1950.[6] Any government concerned for levels of public employment and public expenditure must therefore seek to cut the welfare state.

At the heart of the government's privatisation policy is a set of beliefs and assumptions about the free market. An underlying belief is that the ownership or source of production of a service is vitally important. This is highly debatable. Shackleton, in his meticulous assessment of the case for privatisation, concludes that what offers most benefits is the extension of competition which may or may not involve a transfer of ownership, 'for it must be stressed that transfer of ownership is neither a necessary nor a sufficient condition for greater efficiency'.[7] Many other commentators make the same point.[8]

The free market is also idealised. It is simply assumed that particular situations correspond to ideal type market relationships - and that these relationships are relevant to the production of all goods and services. That is a poor basis for policy. 'Since the claims of the marketeers have always been based upon an image of the market rather than upon its reality', writes Culyer, 'we are inexorably drawn to the conclusion that their analysis is entirely irrelevant'.[9]

A third assumption is that market provision is always more efficient than public sector provision. It is an assumption which is strongly contested. 'There is no systematic evidence', Maynard concludes, 'which demonstrates that the private provision of health care is more efficient than that in the NHS'.[10]

Much play is made by the government over the savings accruing from contracting out; savings which are alleged to prove the greater efficiency of private enterprise. Critics, however, have pointed out that if true comparisons are to be made then the advantages enjoyed by the private contractor need to be clearly recognised - and they are considerable.[11] It may be cost advantages rather than more efficient working practices which help the private contractor. Ascher suggests too that the main reason why contracting out has been successful in local government is that it has been employed by councils with the most scope for gains in efficiency.[12]

A fourth assumption is that in market situations the consumer has much more power. This assumption is underpinned by the notion of the consumer as shopper. The shopper, however, can only buy what is available. She is subject to the vagaries of producers just like the would-be consumer of health care, though she does benefit from a wider range of producers. Returning services to the market does not, however, necessarily produce the greater competitiveness which alone might achieve this.

Fifth, there is the belief that management practice in the private sector is superior to practice in the public sector and that such practices are transferable. In their study *Improving Public Management* Metcalfe and Richards conclude that private sector management practice 'is not a universal panacea. A *Which?* consumer survey would put it in the category of "worth considering" rather than awarding it the accolade of an assured "best buy"'.[13]

Finally, there is the New Right assumption that freedom is enhanced when individuals buy and sell goods and services in market relationships and that it is reduced when services are publicly provided. Such a bald assumption oversimplifies complex issues. The nature of freedom; the value and significance of what is being provided; the terms on which it is being provided; and whether and how it would be provided by the market, are all important considerations but are lost in ideological generalisation.

A number of key assumptions provide the motivation to work for the return of services to market forms of provision. They also underpin a negative reaction to the public provision of welfare. It is depicted as inherently inefficient because it is monopolistic and not subject to the benign influence of competitive markets; as poorly directed to consumer needs because its pattern is determined by self interested bureaucrats and professionals; as inherently inflationary because of the pressure it generates for higher taxes.

Political

The political aims, beliefs and assumptions which have fuelled the government's privatisation policy are very varied. There is a group of what might be called party aims. In 1982 there were immediate party needs when the government's general economic strategy seemed in disarray and the party needed a cause. There was the impetus given by Christopher Chope's Ten-Minute Rule Bill in favour of compulsory tendering in April 1984 which showed the Government the strength of feeling in the party. There was the universal desire within the Conservative Party to do something to weaken the power of the public sector unions who were blamed for wounds inflicted on the Heath Government in 1974.

Secondly, there were the broad ideological views of the New Right - that the state was overgrown and overblown, that big government was a threat to freedom, that government provision created a culture of dependency, that government action always failed to achieve its objectives.

Thirdly, there is the belief in the dead hand of the state, in the inherent inefficiency of public activity and public enterprise, the belief that what the state touches becomes from that moment inefficient. The argument proceeds very smoothly from assertion to assertion. State action is monopolistic. Monopolies are inefficient. Managers of public services have no incentives to efficiency because neither they nor their services are exposed to the disciplines of the market. Therefore they are inefficient. Bureaucrats pervert the aims of service so the stated, official aims are always unobtainable.

These political beliefs lead in two clear directions - a programme of privatisation and the introduction of private sector techniques and approaches where the public sector is retained.

Obviously economic and political aims and assumptions are closely related. Often they are scarcely distinguishable. However, it is important to see privatisation as rooted in immediate political needs and in a political ideology and not just something produced by economic aspirations.

Social

The social aims and assumptions underpinning the drive for privatisation rests on the supposedly debilitating effects on society of government responsibilities. The welfare state is alleged to create dependency; a nation 'hanging on the nipple of state maternalism' as Corelli Barnett inelegantly puts it,[14] which saps vitality, undermines individual responsibility and provides no encouragement to effort or achievement.

The corollary is the moral benefit to a society where individual responsibility is clearly established, and that is to be achieved through expanding private ownership of homes and firms and liberating people from trade union restrictions. Policies with these aims, Brian Griffiths argues, 'constitute a fundamental step forward in the creation of a more responsible and healthy society'.[15]

There is, if anything, less evidence to support the social beliefs used to justify privatisation than there is to support the economic and political assumptions. Advocates simply seize on certain alleged problems of modern society and blame the growth of the public sector as if the links were self evident.

What has happened since 1979

The most dramatic developments in privatisation since 1979 have been the sale of major public enterprises such as British Telecom and British Gas - with electricity and water soon to follow. In 1979-80 asset sales yielded less than £400m. The estimate for the yield in 1988-89 is £5.7bn. Whether greater efficiency will be achieved remains to be seen. What is already clear is that a new popular capitalism has not been created.

The focus here, however, is on developments in welfare services, with what has been done and its significance in particular policy areas. Two general developments have affected all services - the government's attempts to restrain and cut back social expenditure and the policy of extending and increasing charges. They have been a strong pressure for a general privatisation by forcing people to depend on personal, family or other sources of support rather than public services.

Health

In health care it is possible to discern four ways in which the government has encouraged and furthered privatisation.

First, there has been the moral and practical encouragement to the extension of private health insurance. In 1979 some 2.8m people were covered by private health insurance. By 1983 the figure was 6.5m.[16] In 1978 forty four per cent of managers received free health insurance. By 1984 the figure was sixty nine per cent.[17] These developments were encouraged by tax concessions to lower paid individuals and to companies on the cost of private health insurance premiums.

A second factor was the new contracts for consultants introduced in January 1980. All NHS consultants, rather than just those with part time contracts, became entitled to do private work. In Higgins's words, 'the potential for the expansion of private practice was dramatically changed'.[18]

A third aid and comfort to the private sector was the abolition of the Health Services Board in 1980. The Board had been set up in 1976 to monitor and control developments in private medicine. Its abolition was a clear statement of a changed attitude to private medicine.

A fourth element in government policy was the circular of September 1983 instructing District Health Authorities to put certain ancillary services out to tender. By mid 1985, however, nearly half the District Health Authorities had not responded and the House of Commons Select Committee concluded that competitive tendering 'to date has not brought home the bacon'.[19] That was true, but a process of denting the largest public service in Europe had begun. What some supporters of privatisation argue, however, was that tendering did not actually produce the competition which was crucial to greater efficiency.[20]

Housing

The most significant of the government's moves towards the privatisation of welfare has been the sale of council houses - 'in social, political and economic terms, the most important element in the privatisation programme of the Thatcher governments' (Forrest and Murie[21]). By 1987 more than a million dwellings had been sold, with discounts rising to seventy per cent in 1986.

The size of the subsidies suggests very strongly that the main motive was ideological.[22] Sales reduce the number, range and quality of dwellings available in the public sector. The sale of council housing can be seen as an attempt to reassert the principle that housing is a private good rather than a public service. It asserts owner occupation, and by implication the 'residual' nature of public provision, as the norm. It is, as Forrest and Murie put it, not 'a disengagement of the state from the sphere of consumption but a reorientation towards individualised benefits'.[23]

Other developments in housing policy since 1979 have moved in the same direction. The public provision of housing has been cut to enforce the principle of individual private provision. Sharp rent increases for surviving local authority tenants have been designed both to impress on tenants the advantage of not being local authority tenants and to move local authority housing towards a market approach.

Finally, the 1987 Housing Bill aimed to marginalise the role of the local authority as landlord. Private landlords and housing associations are to be encouraged to take over council housing. Tenants will be able to vote to stay with the council or to move to the new landlord, but anyone who fails to vote will be counted as having voted for the new landlord!

Schools

Peacock has pointed out the many practical difficulties involved in privatising schools. The structural and attitudinal changes involved are manifestly greater than those involved in public corporations organised to sell goods and services. Major changes in management would be required. The teaching unions would be very opposed to the change.[24]

The two most significant forays in the direction of privatisation in education have been the Assisted Places Scheme and the 1988 Education Reform Act. The Assisted Places Scheme was designed to enable bright working class children to enjoy the benefits of private education. In fact, the main beneficiaries seem to have been children of 'submerged middle class' parents rather than genuine members of the proletariat. By 1988 some 33,000 pupils were enjoying the subsidy - at a per capita cost greater than the average spending per head in state secondary schools.[25]

The 1988 Education Reform Act allows schools to opt out of local authority control and be funded by central government - 'the Thatcherite core of the Government's Education Reform Bill'.[26] This is not, of course, direct privatisation. As it stands it is no more than an attempt to weaken the control and role of the local authority but it is a clear step towards a more mixed economy of education.

The Act has other elements of more direct privatisation. Charges can be levied for individual music tuition during school time, for board and lodging for residential courses and for activities carried on outside school time. Parents are also to be encouraged to make a larger voluntary financial contribution to their children's school.

Social security

In social security there are three major potential avenues to privatisation - a weakening of the existing state system by restrictions on the range or value of benefits; compulsory private insurance for certain contingencies; and compulsion for employers or other bodies - trades unions for example - to cover certain risks.

Since 1979 Conservative governments have pursued the first and third of these. There has been a long sequence of raids launched against the social security system, culminating in the 1986 Social Security Act. For many groups benefits have become less adequate as a means of protection and provision[27] and people have been forced back on their own private resources. Changes in the state's role in the provision of earnings-related pensions effected in the 1986 Act have merely been the most publicised change. The changes in SERPS are a clear narrowing of state responsibility with the aspiration and assumption that 'restructuring' the state scheme will encourage private sector development.

Since 1983 employers have been responsible for the payment of statutory sick pay. A major historic responsibility of the state was privatised with remarkably little debate or protest. The scheme reduced direct state spending by some £435m in 1983-84 but compensation to employers cost £615m. It was only the £215m recouped in the taxation of sick pay - a change made quite independently of the introduction of the SSP scheme - which allowed the Government to claim cost savings. The figures confirm the point made by Rein and Rainwater that 'the legislation was passed because of its high symbolic value'.[28]

Personal social services

Government policy towards privatisation in personal social services contains three elements. Firstly, from 1980 a range of government ministers including the Prime Minister has stressed the value and extent of the voluntary sector contribution to social welfare. Voluntary organisations have been lauded and courted, given more public money and urged to seek support from commerce and industry.

The government's particular emphasis has been on the centrality of the informal sector. Community care means care *by* the community. The state is not responsible; the personal is not political; the responsibility for care is personal and private. Glowing tributes are paid to carers as the standard bearers of private responsibility, sparing the tax payers the crushing and unmerited burdens of collective responsibility for private ills.

Another policy easy to pursue in personal social services is privatisation by inaction. When resources are not increased in line with new needs, the responsibility for caring is privatised. For example, failure to increase public provision in line with the increasing number of very elderly people is care privatisation. Klein sees this as the government's strategy.[29]

The other key element in the privatising of social care is the grant of public funds for the expansion of private sector provision. It is contributions from the DHSS - probably worth £1bn in 1988-89 - which fuelled the enormous expansion of private residential care in recent years. What is perhaps odd is that while the government is committed to community care as a policy, community care services have been kept desperately short of resources while public money has poured into private residential provision.

Public or Private?

The crucial question, of course, is not 'Public or Private?' More important is the question of *how* we choose between public and private provision and *how* we establish the proper balance between them. What is utterly clear is that the future of welfare is a much more overtly mixed economy than has existed in the past forty years. We are much more into a 'situational ethics' situation of pragmatic decision making. Supporters of 'the pure doctrine of state welfare' - if they ever existed - are in retreat. The welfare pluralists are left camping on the field of battle clutching certain principles with which few would quarrel but whose application remains somewhat uncertain.

Clearly there are areas of welfare provision where it may well be more efficient and effective to ensure people have the money to buy services rather than the public sector provide them. Equally, there are areas where state provision seems the only way to guarantee an acceptable level and pattern of service. At the moment, however, privatisation as a policy feels more like a reaction to the dominance of collective provision and some of its problems than a carefully formulated strategy pointed at certain areas where the arguments in favour of privatisation have been weighed and found convincing.

Predictably views vary on the significance of what has been happening. Greenleaf sees the policy as 'perhaps the most vital aspect of the libertarian resurgence of recent years, a clear and explicit break with the bipartisan consensus prevailing since the second War'.[30] Steel and Heald, writing in 1984, described privatisation as 'rapidly becoming the dominant political issue of the decade'.[31] Peacock, also writing in 1984, recorded his disappointment at 'the marked lack of interest of the present government in privatising the welfare state other than housing'.[32] Those whose focus is primarily on the privatisation of public enterprises see major changes which increasingly have an air of irreversibility about them. Those whose concern focuses on welfare find it less easy to see changes which are obviously epoch-making.

At this stage it is hardly possible either to assess the success or failure of the government's attempts to privatise elements of the welfare state or to establish general criteria to guide the private-public decision across the welfare spectrum. Many of the aims and aspirations which have fuelled the programme are too vague to permit real evaluation - the encouragement of individual responsibility, the reduction of bureaucratic power, the development of more responsive services. Other aims, such as the achievement of greater efficiency, are very complex.

What is possible at this stage is to try to tease out the significance - actual or potential - of the policies the government has been pursuing. Five points are picked out here.

First, the government's policy has distracted attention from really important issues about the provision of public social services. Even those firmly committed to a major role for the state in welfare would agree that there are key issues which must be faced. Questions such as what works in welfare; what doesn't work; how can services be made more efficient, effective and acceptable; and the nature of an efficient, effective and equitable mixed economy of welfare are firmly on the agenda of all students of social policy. Many supporters of welfare state policies would now be prepared to engage, for example, in a discussion about the relative merits of public *funding* of services as an alternative to public *provision*. There is also a fuller realisation of the role and contribution of the voluntary sector. Supporters of state welfare accept the need for debate, discussion and experiment around these issues.

The government's seeming belief that the solution to current doubts and ills is to move from public to private provision bypasses the debates which could and should be taking place about whether and when public provision has advantages, and whether and when private provision should be favoured, and traps them in an ideological cage. 'Privatisation', Maynard insists, 'solves none of the basic health care problems'.[33] Walker makes the same point in his conclusion that 'the privatisation strategy is... at best a diversion from the long overdue task of rethinking the welfare state and, at worst, one that increases the inadequacies of the public social services'.[34]

Secondly, privatisation clearly represents part of a move towards restructuring state involvement in welfare. The state's provider role is reduced. Public money is used to encourage private provision. Regulation of private provision replaces public provision. Tax allowances replace explicit public subsidies. The state still has a role but it is less clear, less explicit, less prominent. The state becomes much less central as a provider, though it may remain highly significant as a source of funds. There is an interpenetration of the public and private sectors with what Rein and Rainwater describe as 'sectoral blurring'.[35]

The supposed 'pure doctrine of state welfare' - public funding and public provision of services to meet all major social needs - is dead. But the crucial question of how we choose the most appropriate pattern of provision has not been properly faced. Restructuring has preceded any establishment of the criteria on which decisions might sensibly be made.

Thirdly, privatisation affects attitudes to welfare. To argue for private provision of services is to make an implicit statement about the individual nature of need and responsibility. In a society which is much richer than the society of 1948 it may be appropriate to re-examine the spheres of individual and collective responsibility. It may well be possible now for the people to meet privately needs which could only be met collectively forty years ago. Even if that were true there might still be a case on broader social grounds for collective provision. Clearly privatisation reflects and influences changes in attitudes but its impact needs very careful assessment. Higgins sketches very clearly a pattern of changes in attitudes to health engendered by a policy of encouraging private provision. She sees the growth of the private sector since 1979 as having 'breached the fundamental principles of health service distribution established after World War II, that services should be allocated according to need rather than to demand or ability to pay'.[36] What we have seen is 'the transition from private medicine as a cottage industry to private medicine as a business enterprise'.[37] This has 'weakened the commitment to equal access to health services for all'.[38] To set against these 'costs' are the substantial benefits which have accrued to some people from the expansion of the private sector.

Fourthly, privatisation clearly has implications for the distribution of services and for social solidarity. The expansion of private pension provision can exacerbate social division in old age while making many old people better off. West emphasises what he calls 'the intertemporal impact' of the growth of private medicine.[39] Those with private insurance during their working lives are unlikely to grasp their future dependence on the NHS so they are unlikely to take steps as voters and taxpayers to ensure it gets the resources it needs. The result will be increased inequalities in health care between younger and older and between those with private insurance and those dependent on the NHS. The policy of selling local authority housing leaves behind the poorest, most disadvantaged tenants in the poorest, most problematic housing. What is developing, according to Forrest and Murie, is provision of generously subsidised individualised state welfare alongside 'a reduced quality, residualised collective provision'.[40]

Fifthly, privatisation is significant in helping to make possible the tax cuts demanded by the government's economic strategy. Privatisation earned the Exchequer some £5bn in 1987-88 which is worth some 4p on - or off - income tax. If cutting taxes is vital to release the nation's energies and retain popular support, and public expenditure cannot be drastically pruned, then privatisation becomes a vital element in basic economic strategy quite apart from its social and political purposes.

The government's privatisation policy marks a major break with the policies of previous governments. It is a response to widely shared concerns about public social service provision. But essentially it is a response based on beliefs rather than on a careful assessment of advantages and disadvantages. There are services which are likely to be provided more efficiently and effectively by the private sector. Equally, there are services which will be better provided by the public sector. The important question is to decide what these various services are.

Those employed in central areas of welfare - doctors, nurses, teachers, social workers, residential care staff, those employed in housing departments - have been involved in the government's privatisation policy in various ways. The willingness of consultants to engage in private practice has made the expansion of private medicine possible, as has the movement of nurses to private hospitals. Social workers have been affected only indirectly by the rapid expansion of private residential care funded by the same Department which was seeking to restrict spending on community services. Teachers are only just beginning to face the possibility offered by the 1988 Education Reform Act of contracting out of local government control to a more private and less public status. Housing department staff have seen the enforced sale of much of the more desirable housing stock, sharp cuts in funds for new building and rising waiting lists - all contributing to a more difficult task.

Opposition to privatisation by welfare professionals has been limited. Privatisation has not confronted them as directly as proposals for contracting out have affected hospital cleaners and caterers and local authority manual workers.

In general, opposition has been muted. What is plain is that there is widespread support in the general population for privatisation and for private health care and private education.[41] Those opposed on principle and because of threats to their jobs are uncertain of public support.

With the notable exception of local authority housing the overall impact of privatisation policies on social welfare remains as yet small. The government's initiatives have been tentative, piecemeal and exploratory. What is scarcely in doubt is that there is more to come. What is scarcely in doubt, either, is that the supporters and opponents of privatisation in social welfare should be pressed to develop the arguments and clarify the issues.

References

1. Rein, M. and Rainwater, L. *Public-Private Interplay in Social Protection*. Sharpe, 1986, 4.

2. Donnison, D.V. 'The Progressive Potential of Privatisation'. In Le Grand, J. and Robinson, R. *Privatisation and the Welfare State*. Allen & Unwin, 1984, 45.

3. Young, S. 'The Use of Subsidies as Part of the Conservative Government's Probation Strategy in Britain 1979-85'. Unpublished paper, 1985.

4. Walker, A. 'The Political Economy of Privatisation'. In Le Grand and Robinson, op. cit., 25.

5. Leat, D. 'Privatisation and Voluntarisation' *Quarterly Journal of Social Affairs*. 2, 3, 1986, 290-291.

6. Rein and Rainwater, op. cit., Ch.1.

7. Shackleton, J.R. 'Privatisation: The Case Examined' *National Westminster Bank Quarterly Review*. May 1984, 70.

8. E.G. Matcalfe, L. and Richards, S. *Improving Public Management*. Sage, 1987, 172.

9. Culyer, A.J. 'The NHS and the Market'. In McLachlan, G. and Maynard, A. *The Public/Private Mix for Health*. Nuffield Provincial Hospitals Trust, 1982, 50.

10. Maynard, A. 'The Private Health Care Sector in Britain'. In Mc?MacLachlan and Maynard, op. cit., 157.

11. Heald, D. *Public Expenditure*. Martin Robertson, 1983, 308.

12. Ascher, K. *The Politics of Privatisation*. Macmillan, 1987, 246.

13. Metcalfe and Richards, op. cit., 175.

14. Barnett, C. *The Audit of War*. Macmillan, 1987, 294.

15. Quoted in Jenkins, D.E. *God, Politics and the Future*. SCM, 1988, 15.

16. Papadakis, E. and Taylor Gooby, P. *The Private Provision of Public Welfare*. Wheatsheaf, 1987, 58.

17. Higgins, J. *The Business of Medicine*. Macmillan, 1988, 94.

18. Ibid, 87.

19. Quoted in Ascher, op. cit. 189.

20. Blundell, J. 'Privatisation by Political Process or Consumer Preference' *Journal of Economic Affairs*. Oct.-Nov. 1986, 60.

21. Forrest, R. and Murie, A. *Selling the Welfare State*. Routledge and Kegan Paul, 1987, 1.

22. Whitehead, C.M.E. 'Privatisation and Housing'. In Le Grand and Robinson, op. cit., 128.

23. Forrest, R. and Murie, A. 'Marginalisation and Subsidised Individualism' *International Journal of Urban and Regional Research*. 10, 1, 1986, 61.

24. Peacock, A. 'Privatisation in Perspective' *Three Banks Review*. December, 1984, 18-19.

25. Papadakis and Taylor Gooby, op. cit., 35-36 and 96.

26. Fairhall, J. 'A Decisive No to Opting Out' *Guardian*. 9 Feb. 1988.

27. Walker, A. and Walker, C. (Eds.) *The Growing Divide*. CPAG, 1988.

28. Rein and Rainwater, op. cit., 208.

29. Klein, R. 'Privatisation and the Welfare State' *Lloyds Bank Review*. January 1984, 25.

30. Greenleaf, W.H. *The British Political Tradition*, Vol. 3. Methuen, 1987, 459.

31. Steel, D. and Heald, D. (Eds.) *Privatising Public Enterprises*. RIPA, 1984, 13.

32. Peacock, op. cit., 18.

33. McLachlan and Maynard, op. cit., 161.

34. Le Grand and Robinson, op. cit., 44.

35. Rein and Rainwater, op. cit., 203.

36. Higgins, op. cit., 222-223.

37. Ibid, 228.

38. Ibid, 237.

39. West, A. 'Private Health Insurance'. In Le Grand and Robinson, op. cit., 114.

40. Forrest and Murie, op. cit., 62.

41. E.g. Taylor Gooby, P. 'Two Cheers for the Welfare State: Public Opinion and Private Welfare' *Journal of Public Policy*, 1982, 2.4.

Planning in a Mixed Economy: Life After Griffiths

Gerald Wistow and Melanie Henwood

Introduction

Perhaps one of the most unexpected developments in health and social care in recent years has been the emergence of a more 'mixed economy', especially apparent in the rapid expansion of private residential and nursing home care. This development has not been inconsistent with the Government's enthusiasm for the market place, but unlike its excited pursuit of privatisation in the economic field, the shift towards a greater diversity of social welfare providers has *not* hitherto been actively planned. All this could now be changing. The Griffiths report on community care published in March 1988[1] presents proposals intended to stimulate the further development of the mixed economy of care, leaving the public sector with a still smaller role in direct service provision.

In what follows we identify some of the implications of this trend for the public sector, and most particularly in relation to its planning role. This issue is especially significant. Successive post war administrations have sought to co-ordinate health and social care within a common planning framework.[2] However, these planning systems took little account of non-statutory welfare which was assumed to be a minimal - if not declining - element of the total care system. Such an approach is clearly inappropriate in a context where the present Government seems intent on promoting 'internal markets' within both health and social services. The question remains, however, to what extent - and how - can a mixed economy of care be planned by the public sector? In addressing this central issue we consider whether Griffiths' recommendation that local authorities should act as the designers and arrangers - rather than monopolistic providers - of care[3] represents an effective mechanism for balancing the development of the market with the responsibilities of the State.

Planning social care

Central Government's enthusiasm for planning health and social care was at its peak a decade ago. With hindsight, it is clear that the years 1976 to 1979 were the high-water mark of attempts to shape the development of health and personal social services within a single comprehensive framework of detailed national guidelines. This period was not, of course, the first in which such national planning exercises were conducted. The old Ministry of Health had initiated ten year plans for hospital services in 1962 and for local authority community health and welfare services in the following year.[4] Subsequently ten year plans for the then newly unified personal social services were launched in 1972 by the Department of Health and Social Security.[5] However, this last set of plans, together with the resource assumption of ten per cent growth a year on which they were based, were almost immediately submerged in the wake of the following year's oil crisis.

The structural reorganisations of health and local government services in 1974 were in no small part intended to sustain more rational and comprehensive planning systems within common local boundaries. Such systems were to be animated by the promulgation of national planning guidelines, the first consolidated statement of which was contained in the 1976 consultative document, *Priorities in the Health and Personal Social Services* (PHPSS).[6] Its publication marked the first attempt to establish a single, coherent set of priorities across both sets of services and to express them in terms of quantified targets to be achieved within specified timescales. Based on a newly developed national programme budget, the central thrust of PHPSS was to secure a shift in the balance of spending between acute hospital and other services. To this end, a range of growth rates was specified for various groups of services and clients over the four years to 1980, and guideline levels of provision (planning norms) were codified across all the major health and personal social services activities.

This modification to the previous ten year planning horizon was intended to produce a planning process which would be more realistic in its resource assumptions and thus more robust in practice. In addition, the publication of planning guidelines and spending priorities was backed by the establishment of planning systems for the NHS (in 1976) and the personal social services (in 1977).[7] While observing the constitutional differences in the accountability relationships of the two services to central government, these systems nonetheless represented mechanisms for transmitting national guidelines downward and local plans upward. The output from these separate planning systems was to be aligned at the local level through joint planning mechanisms.[8] Thus instruments were put in place by which local plans could, in principle, both be influenced by detailed national guidelines and monitored in the extent to which they corresponded with such norms and priorities.

Whether these integrated national and local planning mechanisms could have proved effective was never fully tested. First, the proposed switch in resources met with resistance from the acute sector, and in a revised priorities document - *The Way*

Forward of 1977[9] - it was 'toned down from firm targets to hopeful aspirations'.[10] As the 1977 document itself conceded, the spending priorities were not now to be regarded as 'specific targets to be reached by declared dates in any locality'.[11] Second, the Conservative government elected in 1979 set out, at least initially, to disengage the centre from local services and leave local priority setting to local decision making.

The personal social services planning system was immediately jettisoned (partly because of the volume of cuts proposed for those services)[12] and planning guidance issued in 1981 abandoned all planning norms and targets.[13] Thus there were no longer to be, as Klein has remarked,[14] any benchmarks against which to measure progress towards national policies and priorities. Under pressure from the Treasury and the Public Accounts Committee, however, a new Ministerial team quickly instituted a more centralised system for reviewing performance against objectives set annually for each health authority.[15] However, there was - and there remains - no mechanism for monitoring the planning activities of social services departments and ensuring the compatibility of the latter's plans with those that the DHSS was steering through the health service.[16]

While it was all but inevitable that a government committed to reducing the role of the state should seek to modify planning arrangements of the kind it inherited in the health and personal social services, it should be recognised that the approach which underpinned the priorities and earlier planning initiatives was itself fundamentally deficient.[17] Most particularly, it had proved to be long on specifying resource input and intermediate (service) output levels; but it was correspondingly short on the elaboration of policy objectives, especially as expressed in terms of valued outcomes for service users. The most explicit - not least because they were the most clearly quantified - elements of the national planning guidance were the service norms. Expressed as target levels of provision per capita of relevant population groups (e.g. twenty-five residential places per 1,000 population aged over sixty five), their attainment could all too readily become the principal objective of service planning and development.

Thus the norms tended to discourage flexibility in planning to vary the mix or extend the range of services offered. In effect, much planning activity tended to become a somewhat mechanistic activity whereby growth (which was plentiful in the first half of the seventies) was programmed to meet the planning norms.[18] More fundamentally, they provided little encouragement for authorities to review or define the purpose of such provision in quality of life terms. Indicators of quality are of course both conceptually and methodologically difficult to establish and monitor. Nonetheless, it is scarcely an exaggeration to say that success in planning during the seventies was defined by levels of service production rather than by measures of outcome or impact on the lives of service users and their families.

To summarise, by 1981 the era of what conservative ministers dismissed as 'dirigiste planning'[19] had come to an end. As a result, central government had abandoned responsibility for specifying target levels and mixes of provision across the health and personal social services. Paradoxically, the policy imperative for planning these services as an integrated system remained powerful in the shape of a continuing commitment to promote community care. At the same time, however, planning for community care was becoming a considerably more complex task.

In retrospect, there were a number of reasons why community care planning was a relatively straightforward task in the seventies compared with the late eighties. First, service systems were typically characterised by a narrow range of standardised options. This simplified the planning task, although it also meant that users were offered little choice and that services could be only very imperfectly related to individual needs.[20] Second, health and social services authorities had a virtually exclusive role as the planners, providers and funders of formal care. Non-statutory provision was a marginal element in the totality of services. Third, direct central government funding of the private sector was minimal - see below - and restricted in the case of the voluntary sector to experiments of potential national importance (through, for example, Section 64 of the 1968 Health Service and Public Health Act). The Treasury support for local services was almost entirely channeled through health and local authorities, and the latter were free to supplement such funds to the levels they deemed appropriate or politically prudent.

In the first half of the nineteen eighties, however, this situation was substantially transformed, and the planning task became significantly more complex, if not confused. The range of care options expanded rapidly with the emphasis on tailoring flexible packages of care to the changing needs of individuals.[21] Partly reflecting this, the range of potential statutory service providers was also expanded with housing, education and leisure/recreation services (for example) increasingly recognised as necessary components of community care (a process much stimulated by the normalisation philosophy's emphasis on access to mainstream 'ordinary' services). At the same time, voluntary and - especially - private sector provision was growing rapidly, leaving the statutory sector a proportionately smaller role in service provision. Moreover, it was generally expected (but by no means universally accepted) that the growth of non-statutory provision would continue. Meanwhile, rate capping and grant penalties were making it more difficult for local authorities to supplement central government grants, and central government funding was increasingly available through channels which by-passed health and local authority planning. In particular, funding was provided directly by the Centre to non-statutory services

Privatisation

through, for example, social security, MSC programmes, and central initiatives such as 'Opportunities for Volunteering'.

Therefore, diversity of both provision and providers has become a growing feature of community care services. However, the central characteristic of such diversity is that it has emerged by default rather than by design.[22] Indeed, the uncontrolled and unplanned growth of non-statutory provision has attracted much critical attention, to which the establishment of the Griffiths review by the Government was the ultimate response. Before considering whether Griffiths's subsequent proposals form an appropriate basis for planning a mixed economy of care, we identify some of the difficulties and - especially - the policy contradictions which have flowed from the absence of such planning.

The consequences of unplanned change: a case example

Much of the growth in non-statutory provision has been in private nursing and residential care, although there is also some evidence of expansion of private day and domiciliary services.[23] However, not only are trends in residential care easier to chart, but this is also a field in which the most serious policy conflicts have emerged, and in which - to date - the need for a more coherently planned approach has appeared most strongly.

Table 1: Number of residents aged 65+ by type of home 1976-1986 England

	Numbers (thousands)						% change 1976-1986	per cent annual average change
	1976	1982	1983	1984	1985	1986		
Local authority	99.0	103.7	103.6	102.0	101.5	101.7	+ 2.7	0.3
Private	21.3	35.8	42.1	52.7	66.1	77.6	+ 264	13.8
Voluntary	23.8	26.1	26.5	26.0	25.8	25.1	+ 5.5	0.5
Total	144.1	165.6	172.2	180.7	193.4	204.4	+ 42	3.6

Source: Statistical Bulletin, DHSS, *Personal Social Services for elderly and younger disabled persons England 1976-1986 Bulletin 3/5/88.*

The growth of the private market in residential and nursing home care can be traced from the mid 1970s.[24] The most recently provided Department of Health statistics - presented in Table 1 - show that development of local authority residential accommodation peaked in 1982. At the same time there were parallel increases in residents of private homes; increases which began to accelerate rapidly from 1979.[25] Most of this development took place in residential provision for persons aged sixty five plus. Thus, in just ten years there has been a shift from local authorities providing almost seventy per cent of places (with the remainder spread fairly equally between private and voluntary proprietors), to providing just under half - while the private sector has increased its share to around forty per cent of the market.

It is to be anticipated that the need, or demand, for residential care would rise with the ageing of the population. However, the 1987 Firth report on the funding of residential care[26] concluded that 'only around half of the actual increase occurring in this period might have been expected simply on the basis of these known demographic changes'. Much of this additional growth can be explained by the unplanned, public subsidy to private residential care.

In December 1979 Supplementary Benefit ('Income Support' from April 1988) expenditure on private residential care (i.e., under the payment of board and lodging allowances) was £10m. By 1984 this had reached £200m, £671m in 1987,[27] and an estimated £1 billion in 1988. The numbers of people benefiting from such payments rose over the same period from 12,000 to 90,000. Not unexpectedly the *proportions* of residents in private residential and nursing homes receiving supplementary benefit has also risen.[28] Before 1980 this use of supplementary benefit payments was less systematic, but the 'discretionary arrangement used by a minority'[29] became standardised as part of the board and lodging regulations - fees would be paid for those eligible for SB where they were commensurate with local board and lodging charges. Various attempts at cost control followed, but these have been singularly unsuccessful. For example, in 1983 local limits for charges were introduced, but had the generally inflationary effect of *raising* local fees to such a ceiling. National limits were established in 1985 differing according to the category of care.

The growth in both numbers of elderly people in residential care and in the level of public subsidy to the private system raises fundamental matters for planning. First, public expenditure planning controls have been confounded because social security payments - unlike health and local authority expenditures - are not subject to cash limits. Second, and in consequence, resources are much more readily available to support residential rather than community care, (which *is* primarily financed by cash-limited health and local authority budgets). Third, and as a result, there has been a significant shift in financial responsibility from local to central government. Consequently, local capacities to plan and develop community care have been undermined, despite the Centre's insistence that it continues to attach high priority to that policy objective. Moreover, this shift in financial responsibility to central government, and the consequent growth of public expenditure, has been intensified by local authorities recognising and acting upon the incentives to disengage from subsidising residents. Consequently, there has been a fall in both the numbers and proportion of residents supported (funded) by local authorities. The numbers supported in voluntary and private homes have fallen at an average annual rate of nine per cent - from 20,700 in 1976 to 7,800 in 1986.[30]

Further examples of policy conflicts and perverse incentives concern value for money issues. In contrast to benefits targeted towards community care (Attendance Allowance, and Invalid Care Allowance), no test of disability or dependency is needed when using income support to pay for residential care. Persons fulfilling the financial eligibility criteria for supplementary benefit who choose to enter residential care may have their fees paid (subject to the current ceilings). Whether this represents a cost-effective use of public money is an issue which has attracted much concern.

The evidence concerning unnecessary admissions to residential care (i.e. whether residents actually need such care) is controversial. Research commissioned by the DHSS concluded that there was 'little support for the view that a large number of elderly people are inappropriately placed in private or voluntary residential homes'.[31] However, in reviewing that evidence the Committee of Public Accounts emphasised that if all appropriate services to support people in their own homes had been available, only seventy seven per cent of those admitted would actually have needed care.[32] The DHSS had argued that 'the effect of providing alternative facilities to support claimants in their own homes for longer periods might be to increase rather than reduce public expenditure'. However, the Committee noted that 'they had not undertaken specific research to determine whether this would be so'.

The lack of any test of need for residential care at the level of the individual is paralleled by arguable inefficiencies in the distribution of private (subsidised) care. Private residential homes are not spread uniformly about the country. The greatest concentrations are around the South Coast. This does not merely reflect the larger retired populations who have settled in these areas; there is a *greater relative provision*. The Audit Commission found that the number of elderly residents in private and voluntary homes, per thousand population aged over seventy five, was as high as seventy six in Devon or seventy three in East Sussex, compared with nine or ten per thousand in inland areas. Moreover, further analysis suggested that those areas attracting the greatest Supplementary Benefit expenditure on residential care were those 'where the need for care per person over 75 is, if anything, below average'.[33]

Many of the redistributive effects achieved through RAWP and the Rate Support Grant mechanisms are, therefore being undermined by Supplementary Benefits payments 'channeling public funds to people in some of the better off, least deprived parts of the country'.[34]

The lack of control of Supplementary Benefit board and lodging payments at either a local or central level is thus a concern in terms of financial management, policy, planning and implementation. To these apparently 'perverse' developments must be added further concerns around quality and accountability.

There is arguably a major logical flaw in the use of income support mechanisms for the purchase of care. In giving evidence to the Committee of Public Accounts the DHSS argued that it was a matter for individuals - rather than for the Department - in residential homes to ensure they obtained value for money (i.e. that quality of care and general standards were adequate). The individual in residential care, however, is rarely in a position to assume control of his resources and make informed choices on how they might best be spent. The monitoring of standards in residential and nursing homes is a matter respectively for local authorities and health authorities. There has been much recent adverse publicity concerning conditions in homes (both public and private). Such evidence must challenge the adequacy of registration and regulation procedures to protect residents and should concern the DSS which is paying for expensive, yet apparently (in some cases) substandard, care.

The contradictions and inconsistencies of financial control and accountability between local and central Government are again significant. It is local authorities who are having to pick up the knock-on effects of central Government subsidy of private care with greatly increased registration and regulation responsibilities. Yet the resources to fund the necessary inspection service adequately remain the responsibility of local authorities. Calls for an independent national inspectorate (embracing public, private and voluntary residential *and* nursing homes) are in part a response to this dilemma. They also however, reflect the present inconsistencies and contradictions of local authorities requiring standards from private proprietors which their own public sector facilities may fail to meet.

We have argued, from national and local perspectives, that the care system is out of control. It is out of control in both resource restraint and service development terms. In the latter case concern is focused on the balance and quality of services.

Griffiths: a framework for planning a mixed economy

Our analysis of the growth of private residential care suggests two conclusions. First, that central government has lacked a coordinated set of policies through which community care objectives can be consistently pursued. Second, that the capacity of local agencies to plan and manage care systems as a coherent whole has been substantially undermined by the absence of such a coordinated policy framework. Similar conclusions were central to the Audit Commission's highly critical report on community care and were also broadly reflected in the subsequent report of the National Audit Office. Moreover, they formed the starting point for Sir Roy Griffiths, whose penetrating report set out a framework for the development of a system of 'political and managerial responsibility underpinned by a suitable financial system'.[35]

At the same time, however, Griffiths also envisaged that his proposals would 'encourage a proportionate increase in private and voluntary services as distinct from directly provided public services. This process will aid consumer choice both by encouraging the development of a greater range of services and by increasing competition'.[36] At first sight there may appear to be some element of conflict between the twin objectives of developing a more coherent system for financing and managing community care on the one hand, and promoting a more diversified range of suppliers on the other. In the light of recent experience, the latter objective would seem to imply care systems that are even more difficult to plan and control than at present. Indeed, it raises fundamental questions about how, and if, an increased level of non-statutory services can be incorporated within local frameworks of planning and accountability. More specifically, is it really feasible to encourage choice and competition while also ensuring a more cost effective fit between need and provision within a framework which combines national resource planning and locally appropriate service mixes?

Moreover, one of the apparent lessons of the growth of social security support to residents in private residential care is the need to unify four key functions at local level: planning a balance of local services consistent with national objectives; allocating resources to all care sectors within the framework provided by such local plans; matching services to the assessed needs of individuals; and ensuring quality across the system as a whole. Taken together, these functions might appear to imply a system of detailed planning controls. How could such a prescription be compatible with Griffiths' (and the government's) commitment to greater choice and competition in community care through the vehicle of increased pluralism among providers?

Griffiths' solution to these dilemmas is to separate out responsibility for the provision of services from the responsibility for ensuring that appropriate services are provided and resourced. The latter task has two dimensions. Nationally it is to be fulfilled through a designated minister with responsibility for specifying community care values and objectives, 'consistent with the resources available to public authorities charged with meeting them and for monitoring progress towards their achievement'.[37] Locally, the task falls to social services authorities with a recast role as 'the designers, organisers and purchasers of non-health care services, and not primarily as direct providers, making the maximum possible use of voluntary and private sector bodies to widen consumer choice, stimulate innovation and encourage efficiency'.[38]

Thus social services authorities would be required to adopt a managing agency role, sub-contracting care to a range of non-statutory agencies as well as to 'in house' contractors. Indeed, Griffiths emphasises 'that the onus in all cases should be on social services authorities to show that the private sector is being fully stimulated and encouraged and that competitive tenders or other means of testing the market, are being taken'.[39]

Evidence that such steps had been taken would be among the conditions for the receipt of an earmarked central government grant which would include the 'care' element of existing social security payments to residents of homes in the private and voluntary sectors. By the same token, however, public funding for the independent sector would presumably be available only in so far as provision by the latter corresponded in range, volume and quality with the requirements of comprehensive local plans approved by central government.

In addition, social services authorities would be required to draw up local plans based on the needs they identified in their communities (a task which had effectively been superfluous when local planning consisted of working towards national norms based on fixed ratios of population to services). They would also exercise registration and regulatory functions, including the monitoring of standards in all residential and domiciliary services receiving public funds.[40] The Griffiths Report is not explicit about how this responsibility would be exercised. There is concern that subjecting services to the test of the market would mean narrow cost considerations predominated.

However, in ensuring that local services are consistent with nationally promulgated community care values and objectives, social services authorities would presumably be required to specify quality standards applicable to all care sectors. There is still room for concern about the levels of quality which available resources would permit. Nonetheless, standards setting would become an explicit process nationally, with quality assurance for the first time a required component of the local planning and management task. Indeed, it is the essence of Griffiths' managing agency role that social services authorities should be less preoccupied with the process of service production and correspondingly more engaged in ensuring an appropriate relationship between individual needs and service outcomes.

The Griffiths report can be viewed positively, therefore, as a framework for planning and managing a system which has not hitherto been managed effectively. In effect, it combines elements of a market approach with elements of more traditional rational planning processes. Potentially, indeed, it offers an opportunity to strengthen precisely those components of earlier planning systems which historically have been under-developed: needs identification, objective setting and quality assurance. Whether such a hybrid model could, in practice, constitute an effective mechanism for incorporating non-statutory provision within a national planning framework remains to be proved. However, at least four potential limitations are already clear.

First, it is a framework which wholly applies only to those elements of the independent sector supported by public funds. It will not - and could not - control the volume and balance of care purchased entirely through private means; a sector which occupational pensions and capital from owner occupation can be expected to stimulate. On the other hand, if Griffiths leads to enhanced quality assurance programmes in social services departments, the regulation of the private sector as a whole might be expected to become more effective.

Second, reservations have been expressed about the capacity of either central or local agencies to operate in the new roles which Griffiths has proposed.[41] Local authorities only have limited experience in the community care field of specifying service standards, negotiating contracts and ensuring quality. The kinds of management and financial information systems required to underpin their role as arrangers and purchasers of care are conspicuous by their absence. A major management development exercise would therefore be essential and it will not necessarily take root readily.

Third, a system based on service contracts and competitive tendering might lead to the ossification of service systems, unless social services authorities espouse a positive developmental role and not merely a narrowly regulatory one. Indeed, a by-product of focussing public resources much more substantially through a single agency might be to limit the funds available for innovation.

Lastly, the broader resources issue must be faced. Griffiths has proposed a framework in which the adequacy or otherwise of available resources in meeting service objectives within specified timescales would become more apparent. It remains entirely possible, however, that it will open the way to a much more extensive two-tier system of care in which public support will fund only minimal standards for stigmatised minorities with higher standards found in a flourishing private sector for those whose private means are sufficient to purchase them. Griffiths, itself, is an essentially neutral mechanism which could be used to fund different levels and quality of care. It is, however, a response to the dramatic and continuing increase in public subsidy for purchasing private care through the social security system. It offers an elegant framework for planning in that context. Nonetheless, Griffiths himself confessed to a 'sinking feeling that there is nothing so outdated as to provide today's solution to today's problem'.[42] He suggests a variety of possible initiatives including social/health maintenance organisations, insurance/tax incentives, and occupational welfare developments. However, it is by no means clear that we have begun to grapple with the consequences for public sector planning and service development of such departures from a traditional welfare state framework.

References

1. *Community Care: Agenda for Action*. A report to the Secretary of State for Social Services by Sir Roy Griffiths. HMSO, 1988.

2. Challis, L. et al. *Joint Approaches to Social Policy: Rationality and Practice*. Cambridge University Press, 1988.

3. Griffiths, 1988, op. cit., para. 1.3.4.

4. Ministry of Health. *A Hospital Plan for England and Wales*. Cmnd 1604, HMSO, 1962. Ministry of Health. *The Development of Community Care*. Cmnd 1973, HMSO, 1963.

5. DHSS. *Local Authority Social Services Ten Year Development Plans 1973-1983*. Circular 35/72, 1972.

6. DHSS. *Priorities for the Health and Personal Social Services: A Consultative Document*. HMSO, 1976.

7. DHSS. *The NHS Planning System. 1976*. DHSS. *Forward Planning for Local Authority Social Services*. Circular LASSL (77)13, 1977.

8. DHSS. *Joint Care Planning: Health and Local Authorities*. DHSS HC (77) 17, LAC (77) 10, 1977.

9. DHSS. *Priorities for the Health and Personal Social Services: The Way Forward*. HMSO, 1977c.

10. Brown, R.G.S. 'Accountability and Control in the NHS' *Health Service Journal*. Centre 8 papers 28, October 1977.

11. DHSS, 1977c, op. cit.

12. Webb, A. and Wistow, G. *Whither State Welfare? Policy and Implementation in the Personal Social Service 1979-80*. RIPA, 1982.

13. DHSS. *Care in Action: A Handbook of Policies and Priorities for Health and Personal Social Services*. HMSO, 1981.

14. Klein, R.E. 'Health Policy 1979-1983: The Retreat from Ideology?'. In Jackson, P. (Ed.) *Implementing Government Policy Iniatives: The Thatcher Administration 1979-1983*. RIPA, 1985, 189-207.

15. DHSS, *Health Services Development: The NHS Planning System*. HC (82)6, 1982.

16. National Audit Office. *Community Care Developments*. HMSO, 1987.

17. Webb, A. and Wistow, G. 1982, op. cit., and *Planning Need and Scarcity: Essays on the Personal Social Services*. Allen & Unwin, 1986.

18. Webb and Wistow, 1986, op. cit.

19. Webb and Wistow, 1982, op. cit.

20. Challis, D. and Davies, B. *Case Management in Community Care*. Gower, 1986, chapter 1.

21. Ibid.

22. Wistow, G. 'Increasing Private Provision of Social Care: Implications for Policy'. In Lewis, R. et al. *Care and Control: Social Services and the Private Sector*. Policy Studies Institute, 1986.

23. Midwinter, E. *Caring for Cash: The Issue of Private Residential Care*. Centre for Policy on Ageing, 1986.

24. Laing, W. *Private Health Care 1985*. Office of Health Economics, 1985.

25. Ibid.

26. DHSS. *Public Support for Residential Care: Report of a Joint Central and Local Government Working Party (the Firth Report)*. HMSO, 1987.

27. *Hansard* Written answers. 29 April 1988, Col. 336.

28. Firth, 1987, op. cit.

29. Bradshaw, J. 'Financing Private Care for the Elderly'. In Baldwin, S. et. al. (Eds.) *Social Security and Community Care*. Avebury, 1988.

30. DHSS. Statistical Bulletin. *Personal Social Services for Elderly and Younger Disabled Persons, England 1976-80*. 3/5/88.

31. Bradshaw, 1988, op. cit.

32. Twenty Sixth Report from the Committee of Public Accounts. *Community Care Developments*. HMSO, 1988.

33. The Audit Commission. *Making a Reality of Community Care*. HMSO, 1986.

34. Ibid.

35. Griffiths, 1988, op. cit., para. 5.8.

36. Ibid, para. 4.6.

37. Ibid, para. 6.21.

38. Ibid, para. 1.3.4.

39. Ibid, para. 24.

40. Ibid, para. 6.52.

41. Hunter, D. and Judge, K. *Griffiths and Community Care*. Briefing paper 5, Kings Fund Institute, 1988.

42. Griffiths, op. cit., para.39.

The Privatisation of Long Term Care for Older People: From Public Provision to Public Regulation

Linda Challis

It is important to be clear what privatisation means within the context of care for older people; there are big differences between the private *provision* of care, public *payment* for people in privately provided care, and the public *regulation* of private care. It has become an accepted part of the story of privatisation that the last five years have witnessed substantial growth in the amount of privately provided care stimulated by the payment of fees by the income support system. Less attention has been paid to the effects that the privatisation of provision has had on the public regulatory framework.

This chapter charts the ensnarement of the public authorities in issues about long term care, brought about by the development of the private care industries. More specifically, it examines the way in which the Government has been drawn inexorably deeper into the regulation of long term care through both direct means in the form of registration and inspection procedures, and through indirect means by the manipulation of the income support system. The chapter concludes that privatisation has distracted attention from more fundamental questions as to the kind of care system we should like to see develop, and may have made the realisation of a coherent strategy for care in old age harder to achieve.

The development of the care industries and the growth of public funding

The expansion of private residential care home (RCH) and nursing home (NH) care has been both dramatic and substantial. In 1982 there were about 80,000 places in RCHs and 19,000 places in nursing homes; today there are about 170,000 and 79,000 respectively (Challis and Bartlett[1]). Laing and Buisson[2] have estimated that between 1987 and 1988 alone there was an increase of 14,700 nursing home places in the UK, an increase of twenty nine per cent, and 12,800 residential places, an increase of 8.5 per cent. Whilst it may once have been true that the most substantial growth was in residential care home places, the nursing home industry has made its own push, and it is now estimated that corporate providers are supplying about fifteen per cent of nursing home beds.[2] What we have witnessed in the last five years is the birth of two major care industries.

This expansion should be seen within the context of the steadily rising numbers of very old people in the UK. The ratio of high dependency places in all sectors to people aged seventy five and above has increased from about 1:11 in the early 1980s to about 1:9 in 1988. The private sector now accounts for over forty per cent of high dependency places, whereas in 1982 its share was twenty three per cent. Both the public and voluntary sectors' share of provision has declined.

The amount of public finance devoted to supporting older people in care has indeed risen sharply. The changes to a Social Security Regulation in 1980 began the revolution in private care; the bill for board and lodging, the relevant benefit, rose from £18 million in 1980 to £102 million in 1983 but this too needs to be seen in context.

Before the Government's amendment to the Regulation, people in care could be financed in a variety of ways: by local authority subsidy within one of the authority's own homes; by local authority sponsorship in a private or voluntary home; by the NHS for people in hospital; and by personal income and assets. Until recently the proportion of the population aged 75 and above supported by public finance had remained the same for the previous ten years, at about five per cent. What had changed was that the financial contribution by local government had fallen as local authorities withdrew from sponsorship arrangements, whilst central government's contribution had increased thanks to the modification to Regulation 9. By 1986 the level of central government financial support had risen to about £459m; whereas ten years ago the local authorities had been responsible for financially supporting ninety per cent of older people who received help with their care costs, by 1986 they were supporting sixty per cent with central government filling the gap (Challis[3]). About six per cent of the population aged seventy five and above are now receiving some public financial support for their care.

Whatever view is taken of the events of the past few years one thing is plain: privatisation in the context of care for older people is not synonymous with libertarianism. It may be true that over half of high dependency care is now provided by non public providers, but it is also true that those providers are subject to direct regulation in the form of registration and inspection on a scale not seen before, and to indirect control through the public sector's manipulation of the income support system, a system which currently is paying for forty three per cent of the consumers of private and voluntary care.[2]

The development of direct regulation

The current emphasis on direct regulation is the latest phase in a process which began in the early part of the century. The history of direct regulation can be seen as one of ever widening coverage. The public sector has been forced, sometimes rather reluctantly, into trying to exert control over private care and this process shows no sign of stopping. In fact there is every sign that regulatory scope will continue to be broadened and that there will be greater specification and elaboration of the standards with which homes have to comply.

Nursing homes were subject to public regulation before private old people's homes. When the Nursing Homes Registration Act 1927 was first introduced the principal concern was not with the plight of old people, although that did feature, but with maternity homes and homes offering acute medical services. The Select Committee Report of 1926 which produced the case for controls contains no statistics on the incidence of abuse, but it does contain graphic accounts of the appalling conditions found in some establishments. For example, with 'senile, chronic patients' the Committee noted that:

'They frequently develop bed sores due to prolonged neglect. They are rarely washed. The bed linen in changed at very infrequent intervals, even when soiled. The rooms are verminous. No adequate protection is taken to prevent dissemination of contagious or infections diseases.'

The 1927 Act is important because it provided the model for subsequent legislation of this type. With the benefit of hindsight it can be seen that the Act contained a serious weakness which has had an important effect upon the present system of direct regulation: the Act did not define nursing. This omission probably arises from the fact that the homes causing greatest concern were ones where very specific nursing procedures were employed and it must have seemed good enough to construe nursing as being what nurses did. Furthermore, nursing was only beginning to emerge as a profession, some of the most powerful advocates of the need for regulation were nurses, and the incorporation within the Act of the requirement that qualified nurses should be employed in homes was a help in the emergence of nurses as a distinct professional group (Challis[4]).

Subsequent legislation, most notably Part IV of the National Assistance Act 1948, followed the basic pattern set in 1927. In the intervening years homes catering for frail old people had been set up. They did not call themselves nursing homes and they did not employ nurses. They were therefore exempt from the provisions of the 1927 Act. It was these homes which were drawn into the framework of legislation by the National Assistance Act 1948, a clear example of the widening of regulatory scope.

There were problems in defining old people's homes, problems which were never fully resolved. In the 1948 Act they are a residual category once other kinds of homes, most notably nursing homes, have been ruled out. This lack of a substantive definition is the origin of that grey area in which the debate about what is a nursing home and what is a residential care home takes place. It is from this that the double system of regulation we have today has developed where nursing homes are registered and inspected by District Health Authorities (DHAs) and RCHs are registered and inspected by Social Service Authorities (LSSAs). Having two types of home, neither of which is adequately defined, has provided fertile ground for a flourishing of regulatory specification. It has also assisted the development of separate trade and professional identities. It has also created the need for dual registration, the facility whereby a home can be registered as both a RCH and a NH if it fulfills the registration criteria for both. In the light of studies which have shown there to be a substantial overlap in the kinds of clientele resident in both types of home, the distinction between a nursing home and a residential care home probably owes more to the way in which the regulatory legislation has developed than it does to the nature of the institutions or the kind of care delivered within them.[1]

The history of regulation since 1948 has supported the view that there is continual pressure to widen the scope of regulation. The 1948 Act did not specify the number of people for whom care had to be provided in order that the home become registerable. Moreover since the nature of the service distinguishing a home from a private hotel or guest house was not detailed, there developed a group of homes which evaded regulation and which called themselves boarding houses. This class of home was included in the amended legislation of 1983 as a result of a working party report *At Home in a Boarding House* published by the National Institute for Social Work.[5] But the new legislation and the consolidating Registered Homes Act which followed it in 1984, set the limit for the number of people to be cared for in registerable establishments as four or more, thus excluding homes catering for three or less. It included boarding houses which were providing 'personal care'.

Since the 1984 Act came into force there have been calls for establishments which cater for fewer than four people to be included in the regulations, but so far such calls have been rejected on the pragmatic grounds that such legislation would be unenforceable and would in any case have considerable cost implications. Nevertheless the reliance on the private sector and the willingness of the media and the public sector to publicise abuses in private care suggest that the march of regulation will continue apace. Indeed the proposals made by Sir Roy Griffiths in *Community Care: An Agenda for Action*[6] suggest that direct regulation will receive a good deal of attention in the near future, not least because he has advocated the passing of responsibility for registration and inspection of both kinds of home to the LSSA. If this proposal is implemented it seems unlikely that a distinction between care and nursing could be maintained.

As the private sector has grown, so too has the registration and inspection task of DHAs and LSSAs throughout the country. The numbers of staff involved have increased and the way in which they carry out the registration and inspection role is characterised by its variability from one locality to another. Like any other area of social policy implementation which relies upon different local authorities to put into effect general provisions laid down by central government, authorities interpret the guidance and the codes of practice in different ways. What is more, it is quite clear that the registration and inspection task varies enormously from place to place. Some localities have a large number of homes to monitor whilst others have very few; some have to regulate very specialised facilities in their districts, others do not; some authorities have attempted to develop a more integrated approach in their use of private care, others see little value in working with the private sector. All of this has militated against there being a standard pattern of practice and a standard set of requirements being applied throughout the country. What most authorities do have in common, however, is that their principal concern in registration and inspection is matters of quality. The growth of private care has led the public authorities into greater and greater elaboration of standards in the quest for the definitive recipe for good quality care.

This emphasis on quality has been evident from the early days of the direct regulation of care. Both the National Association of Health Authorities (NAHA) Guidelines and Home Life, the codes of practice which are used in conjunction with the 1984 Act, are, in their different ways, all about quality.[7,8] Considerable investment has been made in the specification of the essentials of good care, and the process continues with the recent publication of a Supplement to the NAHA Guidelines.[9] There are, however, signs that direct regulation will develop beyond issues of quality into other areas. This is another example of the way in which the public sector is being forced to increase its investment in regulation in response to the privatisation of provision. The areas include issues to do with the quantity of provision in a locality, the type of care offered, the charge made for care, the location of care and the integration of it within the existing or developing social and medical infrastructure.

The Griffiths Report has opened the way for a more strategic view to be taken of direct regulation, extending the role of the public sector still further. Opposition to the proposal that it should be the LSSAs who take on full responsibility for registration and inspection has been strongly put by the trade association for NH providers, whilst the LSSAs have welcomed the proposal and see Griffiths as a way of reducing the nursing and medical emphasis in the care of older people. These opposing views are not easily reconciled and may have given added impetus to the idea that there should be a single regulatory authority, independent of both health and local authorities, which would cover all types of residential care. Such an approach would mark a major extension of the role of public control of private care.

It is a paradox of the last few years that the development of private care on a scale which would not have been dreamed of ten years ago has had the effect of involving central and local government more closely than ever before in issues of standards and regulation more generally. The prospects are that this will continue, not only in relation to direct regulation but also by indirect means through the public payment for private care.

Indirect control through public payment for private care

Although there seems to have been no clear intent on the part of central government that funding should be used to control or shape the development of the private sector, it has already had a considerable effect. There is clear evidence of the potential for indirect regulation of the industry through the manipulation of the benefit system. There is clear evidence too that more Government attention has been focussed on ways of funding care for people in old age as a result of the expansion of private care than had hitherto been the case.

The changes to a Social Security Regulation in 1980 began the revolution in private care; in response to the sharply increasing rate of take up of board and lodging allowances throughout 1983 and 1984, the Government tried to devise ways of reducing the flow of funds from central government into the receipt books of private home providers. The new system was first introduced in early 1985. Local discretion about the amount that could be paid in respect of individual residents was removed from Social Security offices and a rate for board and lodging allowances was set which applied throughout the country. There were different rates for nursing homes and for residential care homes, and for homes catering for other client/patient groups. In general the rate for nursing homes was above that for RCHs in recognition of the higher costs associated with employing nurses. The introduction of these changes was not, however, sufficient to control expenditure.

The main cause for concern at this stage was the money flowing towards RCHs rather than the smaller number of claims by people in NHs. The Government set up a working party with the task of finding ways of introducing a system for the financial support of residents in RCHs which would be fair, but which would also have the effect of removing the Government's responsibility for an entitlement, and therefore open ended, benefit. The working party was a joint central and local government group and had the following as its terms of reference:

'To consider the scope for improving collaboration between the Department of Health and Social Security (DHSS) and local authorities in relation to the support of residents in private and voluntary residential care homes, and in particular in the assessment of the need of clients for residential care and in ensuring that charges met from public funds are related to a reasonable standard of provision and represent value for money.'

The report of this group was published in May 1985 and its principal conclusion was that need assessment should be introduced (DHSS[10]). For the longer term the group outlined three options for financing care. The three options were: firstly, to transfer responsibility for residential care in both public and private sectors to the income support system; secondly, to give local authorities the responsibility for financing care costs; and thirdly, to give the DHSS responsibility for the board and lodging element and give the local authorities the responsibility for the care element. These options were referred to another working group for further consideration.

The Firth report was published in July 1987,[11] but by then the seriousness of the situation had been made very clear by the Audit Commission Report *Making a Reality of Community Care*[12] which had estimated the potential bill for residential care with which the Government could be faced as being in the region of 2 billion pounds. Firth recommended that responsibility for funding all residential care costs should pass to the local authorities. The issue of responsibility for nursing home finance was not addressed by Firth; that was referred to the review being carried out by Sir Roy Griffiths.

The Griffiths report recommended a radical realignment of responsibility for the management and the financing of care. In essence the report proposed that the local authorities should take on responsibility for deciding who needs care, when they need it, and who should get funding. Whilst the Government would have to make funds available to the local authorities to carry out this task it would also mean that the Government could exercise control over how much grant the local authorities receive and therefore, indirectly, the amount of private care which is to be supported by the public authorities. The belief that private care was being used by people who did not need such intensive provision, a view which had underpinned the idea that the introduction of needs assessment would limit the Government's financial commitment, was found to be without much substance (Bradshaw and Gibbs[13]). With the publication of the Griffiths Report the question of how to fund care in old age had received more official attention, thanks to the growth of a private sector, than it had received at any time since the creation of the Welfare State.

The importance of the Government being accurate in setting the amounts allowed to local authorities to fund care under a Griffiths scheme, or indeed the importance of the Government being accurate in its setting of benefit levels if it retains responsibility, is very great. There are now substantial numbers of people in private care supported entirely by public funding. Not only that, there are substantial numbers of people in care who were attracted there by the prospect that if their money ran out the bill would be paid by the state. There are substantial numbers of providers who were attracted to the industry for similar reasons. As health and social service authorities dispose of their own provision in order to generate funds to finance shortfalls arising in other areas, a system is being created which relies very heavily upon private individuals and companies. The viability of such a system depends upon the industry's remaining an attractive business proposition. One way in which the industry will become less attractive to existing providers and to potential providers is if the level of public financial support for people in private care drops below an acceptable level.

If, for whatever reason, the Government were to set the level of benefit at a point below that which providers regard as reasonable, allowing for profits, it seems likely that a class of home will develop which will provide only basic, even poor, care. The top end of the market will survive as long as there are people who can afford private care at almost any price, care funded through investments, pensions, and so on. It is possible however that there may not be very much provision catering for people with a middle range income. About one half of the older population are owner occupiers and it is likely that it is this asset wealth which has already fuelled some of the expansion of the care home industries. Capital asset realisation alone is not, however, going to be able to sustain a market which is so structured as to mean that once spend-down occurs, i.e. the money runs out, a person has to move to a cheaper home. Someone who depends upon the cash realised by selling their house probably has enough money to pay for care for three to four years in a middle range nursing home; if the assets are having to support care for two then it is likely to run out within two years. Spend-down, or the prospect of it, is therefore a very real threat for even relatively affluent people. It is this which may make entering a home less attractive, and consequently may constitute a disincentive for providers to provide in the middle range. This is not an encouraging view of the future but it is one which could come about almost by accident if policy on public funding for care is insensitive to the dynamic of private provision.

Perhaps the greatest disservice that the relatively uncontrolled expansion of private care has done for care of older people is that it has made the realisation of a coherent system of care much more difficult to achieve. It can be argued that this area of policy is experiencing the worst of a lot of worlds. From the point of view of the providers there is a burgeoning of quality regulation which seems divorced from any consideration of the costs of providing good quality care, and which are perceived as a series of exhortations to raise standards without any serious attempt by the public authorities to provide the long term investment in staff which is needed to bring about good care. From the point of view of the consumers a system is developing which will be determined by capacity to pay, accidents of geographical location, and which is not equipped to provide users with independent safeguards. At the same time the trade associations and medical, nursing and social professional groups are becoming more fixed in their appreciation of what is and what is not in their interests. This renders it more difficult than ever to engage people in debate about what are the constituents of a good care system. Ascher[14] has argued that the Government's enthusiasm for privatisation was due in part to its determination to see the power of the public sector unions broken. It may have been rewarded in that respect, but their place is being taken by other powerful groups. In view of these developments it is at least worth asking whether the privatisation of care for older people has been of benefit for the consumer; has there, for example, been an increase in choice, a raising of standards?

Privatisation and the consumer

There seems to be a general consensus amongst DHA and LSSA staff that increased quality regulation has brought about an improvement in basic standards. There seems also to be agreement that the standards required of the private sector are forcing the public authorities to look again at the standards which prevail in their own establishments. To that extent the rise of the private sector has had good effects. The obverse of this is, however, that as standards improve we can expect costs to rise and charges to go up, so that access to this better quality care may come to be limited to those who can pay for care without recourse to public subsidy.

The balance sheet as far as choice is concerned is less encouraging. Challis and Bartlett[1] concluded that choice can mean several things in this context: choice about when to enter care, choice about where to have care, choice about a particular home, choice about whether to stay in a particular home. The study of nursing homes which they conducted suggested that for a few people the existence of a private sector did indeed allow a greater exercise of choice in all these respects, but that this was true for only a very small minority of patients. Probably only about four per cent of patients had exercised their right to choose by changing home; probably fewer than ten per cent chose to change locality when they entered a home. Most important in this was the condition of patients - they were not in a good physical or mental state - and the lack of alternative care in homes or in the community presented formidable constraints to the exercise of choice. Most patients were substantially impaired in some way and this is supported for RCHs by the evidence of the York studies.[13] This is not a market in which the notion of consumer sovereignty and shopping around has much validity in practice.

Privatisation

The proposals in the Griffiths report for making community care a reality could be construed as reinforcing the idea that residential care is a last resort. Leaving entry to the last possible moment works against the consumer being able to make a reasonably well informed decision about when and where to enter care. It has long been acknowledged that it is better to bring services to people rather than the other way round; better on humanitarian grounds, better in terms of effectiveness, better in terms of minimising the disruption of existing care arrangements. The danger is that the growth of the private sector will make it harder to create a system which really does allow people a degree of choice about when, where, and what kind of care they wish to receive. To that extent the privatisation of the provision of long term care for older people may represent several steps backwards rather than a leap forward into a brave new world.

References

1. Challis, L., and Bartlett, H. *Old and Ill: Private Nursing Homes for Elderly People.* Age Concern Institute of Gerontology Reseach Paper No. 1, Age Concern England, Mitcham, 1987.

2. Laing and Buisson. *Care of Elderly People: The Developing Market for Nursing and Residential Homes and Related Services in Britain.* Laing and Buisson Publications Ltd, 1 Perren Street, London NW5 3ED, 1988.

3. Challis, L. 'Robbing Peter to Pay Paul - Handsomely' *Social Services Insight.* Aug. 16, 12-14, 1986.

4. Challis, L. 'Controlling for Care: Private and Voluntary Homes Registration and Inspection - a Forgotten Area of Social Work' *British Journal of Social Work.* 15, 1985, 43-56.

5. National Institute for Social Work. *At Home in a Boarding House.* Report of an Independent Working Group, London, 1981.

6. Griffiths, Sir R. *Community Care: An Agenda for Action.* HMSO, London, 1988.

7. National Association of Health Authorities. *Registration and Inspection of Nursing Homes: A Handbook for Health Authorities.* NAHA, Birmingham, 1985.

8. Centre for Policy on Ageing. *Home Life: A Code of Practice for Residential Care.* CPA, London, 1985.

9. National Association of Health Authorities. *Registration and Inspection of Nursing Homes: A Handbook for Health Authorities, 1988 Supplement.* NAHA, Birmingham, 1985.

10. DHSS. *Supplementary Benefit and Residential Care: Report of a Joint Central and Local Government Working Party 1985.* DHSS, London, 1985.

11. DHSS. *Public Support for Residential Care.* DHSS, London, 1987.

12. Audit Commission. *Making a Reality of Community Care.* Audit Commission, London, 1986.

13. Bradshaw, J. and Gibbs, I. *Public Support for Private Residential Care.* Avebury, Aldershot, 1988.

14. Ascher, K. *The Politics of Privatisation.* Macmillan, London, 1987.

The Characteristics of Non-Statutory Residential and Nursing Homes

Robin Darton and Ken Wright

Introduction

During the autumn of 1986 and the spring of 1987, the Personal Social Services Research Unit at the University of York conducted a national survey of private and voluntary residential care and nursing homes. The survey was commissioned by the then Department of Health and Social Security as one of a number of research studies into the payment of supplementary benefit to residents and patients in non-statutory residential and nursing homes and in particular acted as a more detailed follow-up to the survey conducted by Ernst and Whinney in 1985 which examined the relationship between charges and costs.[1] The specific aims of the study were to examine the differences between categories of registered private and voluntary residential care and nursing homes in relation to charges, facilities and resident characteristics and to carry out a preliminary investigation of the hotel ('living') and dependency ('care') elements in charges and costs for residents with varying characteristics in different categories of home. The survey was designed to be compatible with an earlier survey of local authority, voluntary and private residential homes for elderly people, conducted by the PSSRU in twelve local authorities in England and Wales in 1981. The 1981 survey is described in Darton and Knapp.[2] Following the 1981 survey, a subsequent interview survey of proprietors was conducted in 1982 and early 1983 in one-third of the respondent private homes.

In the 1981 survey comparative information was collected on the facilities provided and the characteristics of residents in the three sectors,[3] and the survey provided information for analyses of the factors associated with variations in the costs of local authority homes.[2] The survey, together with the interview follow-up, also provided information for analyses of the factors associated with variations in the charges of private homes.[4] Using the equation estimated by Darton and Knapp for predicting the operating costs of local authority homes, Judge et al. were able to compare the charges of private homes with the predicted costs which they would have incurred if the cost relationship for local authority homes applied to them, allowing for differences in the characteristics of residents, homes and areas. Judge et al. found that the operating costs predicted for private homes were substantially higher than their charges, whereas in the reverse exercise the charges predicted for local authority homes were slightly lower than their operating costs. Although the 1981 survey did not collect data about the final outputs for residents in terms of psychological well-being and quality of life (see Davies and Knapp[5]), Judge et al. felt that the assumption that the two sectors were producing similar consequences for residents was reasonable, and concluded that private residential care represented 'good value for money'.

Similar analyses of factors associated with variations in charges to those undertaken with the 1981 data are being done using the data from the PSSRU/CHE survey in order to tackle the study's second objective. This paper presents information relevant to the first objective of the study together with comparative information collected for residential homes for elderly people in the 1981 survey and in the 1970 Census of Residential Accommodation[6] and also the (unpublished) 1971 DHSS sample survey of private homes.

The PSSRU/CHE survey included residential care and nursing homes and covered establishments catering for the four numerically most important client groups: elderly people, people with a mental handicap, people with a mental illness and people with a physical handicap. However, the majority of nursing homes included in the survey included elderly people among their clientele, as may be expected from national statistics. The number of beds for long-stay elderly patients in England and Wales in 1986 reported in table 5 below represented 68 per cent of the total number of beds in private hospitals, homes and clinics. With the exception of the study by Ernst and Whinney, previous studies of residential care and nursing homes have concentrated on establishments for elderly people. Similarly, few studies (with the exception of the Ernst and Whinney survey and small-scale studies such as those by Challis with Day[7] and Wade et al.[8]) have collected information about both residential care and nursing homes. The PSSRU/CHE survey provides an opportunity for comparing residential care and nursing homes and for comparing homes for different client groups.

The rest of this paper is organised in three main sections plus a summary, covering a description of trends in levels of provision; a description of the PSSRU/CHE survey; comparisons of the facilities provided and the characteristics of residents and patients in the homes in the PSSRU/CHE survey; and comparisons between the data collected in the 1986 survey and the data collected in the 1970/71 DHSS exercises and the 1981 PSSRU survey.

National trends in levels of provision

Tables 1 to 5 present information on the number of registered residential and nursing homes in England, Wales and Scotland for selected years, drawn from national statistics. The inclusion of information for particular years has been partly dictated by availability, although the information presented in tables 1 and 2 has been selected to correspond to the years in which the 1970 DHSS Census of Residential Accommodation, the 1981 PSSRU survey and the 1986 PSSRU/CHE survey were undertaken.

Table 1 illustrates the substantial increase, of approximately 140 per cent, in the number of private residential homes and places for elderly people and people with a physical handicap during the period 1981 to 1986. It also shows that private provision had grown during the preceding five years by approximately fifty per cent, indicating that the more recent rapid growth had built on an existing trend. In the local authority sector the number of homes had risen during the period 1970 to 1976 by eighteen per cent, with a concomitant increase of fourteen per cent in the number of residents, but then showed very modest growth; a total of 103 homes, less than one for each local authority, between 1976 and 1981. Since 1981 there has been a very small increase in the number of homes and places, and a slight fall in the number of residents in 1986 compared with 1981. In the voluntary sector some growth occurred between 1976 and 1981 but the number of homes, places and residents declined between 1981 and 1986. Between 1981 and 1986 private homes virtually doubled their contribution to the total number of places available, from twenty to thirty eight per cent.

In Scotland the private sector has not developed to the same extent as in England and Wales. Registered homes accounted for forty one per cent of the total number of places in homes in Scotland in 1986, compared with thirty eight per cent of places accounted for by private homes alone in England and Wales. The registered home sector in Scotland experienced a seventeen per cent increase in the number of places during the period 1981 to 1986, but in the preceding five years it had remained virtually static, following a previous increase of twenty one per cent in the number of places between 1970 and 1976. The local authority sector in Scotland experienced similar growth during the 1970s to that in England and Wales, but further modest growth has taken place since 1981.

Larder et al.[9] suggest that levels of institutional provision are most appropriately calculated in relation to the population aged seventy five and over. The growth in the number of elderly people aged seventy five and over in England, Wales and Scotland, from figures in the Monthly Digest of Statistics,[10] was thirteen per cent between 1971 and 1976, fifteen per cent between 1976 and 1981, and thirteen per cent between 1981 and 1986. Comparisons between the change in the number of elderly people in the population as a whole and the change in the number of elderly people in residential homes reveals that in England and Wales the growth in the number of residents approximately matched the growth in the number of elderly people aged seventy five and over in the population as a whole during the period 1971 to 1981, but that between 1981 and 1986 the growth in the number of residents was approximately double the growth in the number of elderly people aged seventy five and over in the population as a whole.

In Scotland the number of residents and the number of elderly people aged seventy five and over in the population as a whole grew at similar rates between 1971 and 1976, but after 1976 the growth in the number of residents was much lower than the growth in the number of elderly people aged seventy five and over in the population as a whole. During the period 1971 to 1986 a smaller proportion of elderly people were accommodated in residential homes in Scotland than in England and Wales. In 1971 residents in homes in England and Wales formed approximately 6.0 per cent of the elderly population aged seventy five and over, compared with 5.4 per cent in Scotland, and in 1986 the figures were 6.6 per cent for England and Wales and 5.0 per cent for Scotland.

Changes in the levels of private residential provision for people with a mental handicap or a mental illness in England during the period 1977 to 1986 have mirrored those observed for homes for elderly people and people with a physical handicap, with homes for people with a mental handicap growing even more rapidly during the period 1980 to 1986. However, growth also occurred in the local authority and voluntary sectors between 1977 and 1986. Comparable information is not available for Wales, since figures for private and voluntary homes are not disaggregated by client group. In Scotland levels of growth have been more modest, and recent changes in definitions have affected the comparability of the figures over time, particularly for homes for people with a mental illness. For homes for people with a mental handicap overall levels of growth have been more modest than in England but, as in the case of residential homes for elderly people and people with a physical handicap, the local authority sector has grown more and the independent sector has grown less than in England. Between 1980 and 1986 the number of places in local authority homes for people with a mental handicap in Scotland grew by fifty four per cent, compared with thirty one per cent in England, while the number of places in registered homes in Scotland grew by thirty four per cent, compared with 130 per cent in private and voluntary homes in England.

Less information is available for the nursing home sector than for residential homes, and Larder et al.[9] have reported that the data collected from district health authorities by the DHSS may not be very reliable. Table 5 summarises the information collected by the DHSS and the Welsh Office for 1982 to 1986. According to these figures the number of long-stay places available for elderly patients has increased by twenty to twenty five per cent annually between 1982 and 1986. In 1986 the total number of places in registered nursing homes and residential homes for elderly people and people with a physical handicap in England and Wales, excluding places in residential homes occupied by residents aged under 65, was approximately 290,000; equivalent to 8.8 per cent of the population aged seventy five and over.

The characteristics of residential and nursing homes, staff and clients

Introduction

The PSSRU/CHE survey was conducted in 1986/7 in a sample of 855 establishments in seventeen local authority areas in England, Scotland and Wales, and the results in this chapter are for the 555 homes who responded in full (for technical details, see appendix 1). Table 6 presents information from the survey on the characteristics of homes and their staff, and table 7 presents information on the characteristics of their residents and patients.

Sizes of homes

On average, nursing homes were larger than residential homes in both the private and voluntary sectors, and voluntary homes were larger than private homes. The smallest residential homes were generally those catering for people with a mental handicap or a mental illness, and the differences in the sizes of private and voluntary homes for these client groups were smaller than for other residential homes. Forty one per cent of homes in the private sector and thirty five per cent of homes in the voluntary sector catering for people with a mental handicap had less than ten beds available, and thirty per cent of homes in the private sector and twenty per cent of homes in the voluntary sector catering for people with a mental illness had less than ten beds available. In contrast, seventeen per cent of private residential homes for elderly people and sixteen per cent of private residential homes for people with a physical handicap had less than ten beds available, and three per cent and zero per cent respectively of voluntary homes had less than ten beds available. The corresponding figures for nursing homes were six per cent and seventeen per cent, but there were only twelve voluntary nursing homes. The average size of the voluntary nursing homes was thirty six available beds, compared with twenty six beds in the private sector.

Occupancy rates

The mean occupancy rate for all types of home was approximately ninety per cent. Nursing homes tended to have higher mean occupancy rates (ninety three per cent for all nursing homes) and voluntary residential homes for people with a mental han-

Privatisation

dicap tended to have lower mean occupancy rates (eighty five per cent). With the exception of voluntary residential homes for people with a mental illness, median occupancy rates ranged from ninety four to 100 per cent, reflecting a skew in the distribution of occupancy levels to higher occupancy levels and the existence of establishments operating at substantially lower occupancy levels.

Length of time the proprietors or organisation had been running the home

The proportion of private homes run by proprietors who had recently acquired the home was higher than the proportion of voluntary homes which had recently been acquired by the managing organisation. The proportion of private homes which had been acquired by 1980 ranged from seventeen per cent to forty one per cent, compared with between forty four per cent and 100 per cent of voluntary homes, while the proportion of private homes which had been acquired since 1983 ranged from thirty one per cent to sixty three per cent, compared with between zero per cent and twenty three per cent of voluntary homes.

The availability of a lift and the number of storeys

In both the private and the voluntary sectors more residential homes for elderly people, residential homes for people with a physical handicap and nursing homes had a lift or a single storey for residents or patients than residential homes for people with a mental handicap or a mental illness, as might be expected from the information on the characteristics of residents and patients presented below. For these more physically dependent groups, voluntary homes were more likely to provide a lift or only use one storey for residents and patients, although more problems of mobility occurred among elderly people and people with a mental handicap in private homes than in voluntary homes. In addition it may be noted that thirty eight per cent of private nursing homes were reported as having more than one storey but no lift, compared with thirty two per cent of private residential homes for the elderly, despite the greater levels of physical disability in nursing homes.

Bedroom sizes

Bedroom sizes and the associated cost implications have proved to be particular sources of disagreement between the proprietors of private residential homes and registration authorities. The 1973 DHSS Building Note for residential accommodation for elderly people[11] recommended that most of the beds in residential homes for elderly people should be in single rooms, with a maximum of twenty per cent of beds in double rooms, and the Code of Practice for Residential Care[12] stated that single rooms would normally be considered preferable to shared rooms and that special reasons should apply if more than two people occupied a room. There are no specific recommendations for bedroom sizes in nursing homes.[13] The 1973 Building Note superseded the 1962 Ministry of Health Building Note which indicated that at least forty to fifty per cent of beds should be in single rooms, thirty to forty per cent in double rooms, and no more than ten to twenty per cent (the maximum recommended size) in four-bedded rooms.[14]

The mean bedroom size was approximately 1.6 beds per room for each type of home, although voluntary homes had higher proportions of beds in single rooms than private homes, with the exception of residential homes for people with a mental illness. The largest proportion of single bedrooms for any type of home was fifty seven per cent among voluntary residential homes for elderly people. In both the private and the voluntary sectors, residential homes for elderly people, residential homes for people with a physical handicap and nursing homes provided a higher proportion of beds in single rooms than did residential homes for people with a mental handicap or a mental illness, and a higher proportion conformed to the recommendations in the 1962 and 1973 building notes. Nursing homes and residential homes for elderly people provided a similar proportion of beds in single rooms but nursing homes provided fewer beds in double bedrooms and more beds in rooms with three or more beds. Overall, thirty four per cent of voluntary residential homes for elderly people and twenty seven per cent of voluntary residential homes for people with a physical handicap conformed to the 1973 recommendations, compared with under twenty per cent of other voluntary homes, and with eight per cent of private homes, ranging from two per cent of residential homes for people with a mental illness to ten per cent of residential homes for elderly people.

Bathroom and toilet facilities
Both the 1962 and the 1973 building notes recommended that at least one bathroom be provided for every fifteen residents; the earlier building note recommended a minimum of one WC for every six residents and the later building note recommended a minimum of one WC for every four residents. The Code of Practice for Residential Care followed the recommendations of the 1973 Building Note for the level of WC provision, but recommended that the minimum level of bathroom provision should be one bathroom for eight residents. For nursing homes the National Association of Health Authorities's *Handbook for Health Authorities* commended the same level of bathroom provision as the Code of Practice for Residential Care, but a lower level of WC provision. The recommended level of WC provision was one for every eight patients or one combined WC and bathroom for every six patients.[15]

The mean level of WC provision ranged from 2.8 beds per WC in voluntary residential homes for people with a mental handicap to 3.7 beds per WC in private nursing homes, and the mean level of bathroom provision ranged from 4.1 beds per bathroom in voluntary residential homes for people with a mental handicap to 7.2 beds per bathroom in voluntary residential homes for people with a physical handicap. Nursing homes were less likely to meet the building note standards for WC provision than were the other types of home, as may be expected from the different recommended level of provision. Sixty six per cent of nursing homes met the 1973 Building Note standard, compared with eighty two per cent of residential homes, and eight per cent of nursing homes fell below the 1962 Building Note standards, compared with two per cent of residential homes. Only five respondent homes in the total sample were recorded as having fewer bathrooms than recommended by the building notes, while the proportion of homes which had fewer bathrooms than the minimum of one bathroom for every eight beds recommended by the Code of Practice and the National Association of Health Authorities ranged from twelve per cent of residential homes for people with a mental handicap to twenty two per cent of residential homes for people with a physical handicap. Seventeen per cent of all residential homes and thirteen per cent of nursing homes had fewer bathrooms than the minimum number recommended by the Code of Practice and the National Association of Health Authorities.

Common rooms and dining rooms

Only five homes did not have at least one common room or sitting room. A larger proportion of homes did not have a dining room, particularly among nursing homes. Six per cent of residential care homes did not have a dining room, compared with thirty nine per cent of nursing homes.

Staffing levels

In order to compare the relative contributions of time by staff in different categories the normal working week of thirty nine hours in local authority residential homes[16] was used as the base for calculating whole time equivalents. Hours in excess of eighty four hours, which were recorded chiefly for proprietors of private homes, were arbitrarily truncated to eighty four hours for the purpose of calculating whole time equivalents and staff ratios.

As may be expected, a higher proportion of the staff of nursing homes were qualified nurses, compared with staff in residential homes. Seventeen per cent of staff in voluntary homes (twenty five per cent of the whole time equivalent staff) and twenty seven per cent of staff in private nursing homes (twenty four per cent of the whole time equivalent staff) were qualified nurses, compared with nine per cent of staff in residential homes (twelve per cent of the whole time equivalent staff in voluntary homes and nine per cent in private homes). In addition, eighty seven per cent of private nursing homes included qualified nurses among the proprietors, compared with fifty four per cent of private residential homes. Very few nursing homes employed care staff with a recognised social work qualification (CQSW, CRSW or CSS), and only four per cent of staff in voluntary residential homes and six per cent in private residential homes were qualified care staff. However, residential homes for people with a mental handicap or a mental illness employed similar proportions of qualified nursing and care staff, whereas residential homes for elderly people and people with a physical handicap employed more qualified nurses than qualified care staff. A minority of private homes included qualified social workers among the proprietors, but the proportion was higher among residential homes (ten per cent) than among nursing homes (four per cent).

Proprietors and members of their families accounted for thirteen per cent of the staff of residential homes and for five per cent of the staff of the nursing homes (which were generally large), but accounted for twenty one per cent of the computed whole time equivalent staff for residential homes and ten per cent for nursing homes. Conversely, with the exception of voluntary residential homes for people with a mental illness, volunteers and unclassified staff accounted for less than three per cent of hours worked in all types of home.

Staffing ratios in nursing homes were higher than in residential homes, but varied considerably between the various types of residential home, from a mean of fifteen hours per place per week in voluntary homes for people with a mental illness to a mean of thirty two hours per place per week in voluntary homes for people with a physical handicap. Staffing ratios based on employees, excluding the time of proprietors and members of their families in the calculations for private homes, were lower in private homes than in voluntary homes, with the exception of residential homes for elderly people and people with a mental illness. However, including the time of proprietors and members of their families, assuming an arbitrary maximum of eighty four hours per week, produced staffing ratios which were higher in private homes than in voluntary homes, with the exception of residential homes for people with a physical handicap. This is consistent with the information on the dependency characteristics of residents and patients presented below.

As may be expected from the information on the contribution of proprietors and members of their families presented above, the inclusion of proprietors in the calculation of staffing ratios had the least effect on the staffing ratios of private nursing homes. Other studies of residential and nursing homes have reported an inverse relationship between staff ratios and home size.[17,18,19] Allowing for economies of scale in staffing ratios would increase the difference between staffing ratios in nursing homes and residential homes. Voluntary residential homes for elderly people and people with a physical handicap were larger than other residential homes; allowing for economies of scale would also raise the staffing ratios in these homes relative to those in other residential homes. Further analysis along the lines of the work by

Knapp[20] will be necessary to explore the relationship between staffing ratios and home and resident patient characteristics.

Sex distribution of residents and patients

Table 7 shows that four-fifths of the individuals in nursing homes and in residential homes for the elderly were female, whereas there were similar proportions of males and females in residential homes for the other client groups, although there were differences in the sex-ratios between private and voluntary homes. Such differences were found in nursing homes and in residential homes for people with a mental illness or a physical handicap, and in each case the voluntary homes had a higher proportion of male residents than did the private homes. Thirty per cent of patients in voluntary nursing homes were male, compared with sixteen per cent in private homes. Sixty one per cent of residents in voluntary residential homes for people with a mental illness were male, compared with forty per cent in private homes, and the corresponding figures for residential homes for people with a physical handicap were fifty three per cent and thirty one per cent.

Age distribution of residents and patients

In the private sector the average age of patients in nursing homes (82.4 years) was almost identical to that of individuals in residential homes for elderly people (82.3 years), but in the voluntary sector the average age of patients in nursing homes was substantially lower than the average age of people in residential homes; 73.9 years compared with 83.4 years. As explained in section 3.2 above, private residential homes classified for people with a physical handicap were largely catering for elderly people and this is reflected in the average age of the residents of these homes, 76.8 years. Private residential homes for people with a mental illness also accommodated an older group of individuals than voluntary homes, the average age of residents in these private homes being 65.6 years. In the private sector, only the residential homes catering for people with a mental handicap accommodated individuals with an average age below pensionable age, and the average age of residents in this group of homes (46.0 years) was still greater than that for voluntary homes for the same client group (35.9 years).

Length of stay of residents and patients

With the exception of residential homes for people with a mental illness, the mean lengths of stay for private homes were substantially shorter than those for voluntary homes, but differences in the mean lengths of stay of male and female residents and patients were not consistent across the types of home. The shortest mean lengths of stay occurred among residents in private residential homes for elderly people (twenty two months), private residential homes for people with a physical handicap (twenty three months) and private nursing homes (twenty five months), and the longest in voluntary residential homes for people with a physical handicap (ninety seven months) or a mental handicap (110 months).

Source of admission of residents and patients
With the exception of residential homes for people with a mental illness, the source of admission varied between private and voluntary homes. Private homes had a higher proportion of former hospital patients (thirty nine per cent of residents of private residential homes and forty five per cent of patients in private nursing homes), whereas voluntary homes contained a higher proportion of people who had previously been living at home (fifty five per cent of residents of voluntary residential homes and fifty one per cent of patients in voluntary nursing homes). Sixty per cent of residents in both private and voluntary residential homes for people with a mental illness were previously in hospital. Residents of residential homes for elderly people were most likely to have been living alone prior to entry to the home (fifty two per cent of residents in voluntary homes and thirty three per cent of residents in private homes), and residents of voluntary residential homes for people with a physical handicap were most likely to have been living at home with other people (forty per cent). Thirty eight per cent of residents of voluntary homes for people with a mental handicap had been living at home with other people, but residents of both private and voluntary homes for this client group were more likely than residents and patients of other homes to have been admitted from another home (thirty eight per cent of residents in voluntary homes and thirty per cent of residents in private homes).

Dependency characteristics of residents and patients
Information collected on the individual questions relating to the dependency of residents and patients is presented in table 7, together with the Index of Independence in Activities of Daily Living[21,22] and a measure of aggregate dependency, originally developed for the 1970 Census of Residential Accommodation.[6] The Index of ADL is based on six self-care functions, bathing, dressing, toileting, transfer, continence and feeding, and is calculated from the number of functions with which individuals required assistance, plus two summary measures. The aggregate measure is based on mobility, continence, mental state (confusion) and the capacity for self-care in washing, bathing, dressing, feeding and using the toilet, and is defined by Davies and Knapp.[23]
    The level of physical disability among patients in nursing homes was substantially higher than among people in residential homes, mental confusion was more prevalent in nursing homes than in residential homes, and a higher proportion of nursing home patients exhibited a dependent attitude towards help, defined as generally

wanting things to be done for them. In the private sector, behavioural and psychological problems were more prevalent in residential homes for people with a mental handicap or a mental illness than in other types of home. However, in the voluntary sector behavioural problems were more prevalent only in residential homes for people with a mental handicap, and anxiety (but not depression) was more prevalent only in residential homes for people with a mental illness. The difference from other types of home was less pronounced in each case. As noted above, the majority of nursing homes included elderly people among their clientele, and comparing the patients in nursing homes with the residents in residential homes for elderly people indicates that nursing home patients were generally less mobile, less able to care for themselves, less continent and, in the private sector, more confused:

- ten per cent of voluntary and fourteen per cent of private nursing home patients could walk at least 200 yards outdoors, compared with 46 per cent in voluntary and 36 per cent in private residential homes for elderly people.
- 22 per cent of nursing home patients were chair- or bedfast, compared with three per cent of people in voluntary and four per cent in private residential homes.
- 79 per cent of voluntary and 86 per cent of private nursing home patients were unable to undertake any of six self care tasks, compared with 60 per cent of people in voluntary and 68 per cent in private residential homes.
- 40 per cent of nursing home patients were incontinent, compared with sixteen per cent of people in voluntary and nineteen per cent of people in private residential care.
- fourteen per cent of voluntary and 25 per cent of private nursing home patients were severely confused, compared with twelve per cent of people in voluntary and seventeen per cent in private residential homes.

As noted above, few studies have collected information about both residential and nursing homes. The report by Wade et al.,[8] which was based on a small number of homes in five local authorities, is an exception and produced similar findings on the relative levels of dependency in private residential and private nursing homes. Discussions of the residential and nursing home sectors frequently refer to variations in levels of dependency between homes and individuals,[9] and such variations are concealed in the overall levels of dependency reported for residential and nursing homes. Variations in dependency levels between residential homes for elderly people tended to be greater than for nursing homes, a result which lends support to the response of the Social Care Association to the Wagner Committee's report, that 'many residents at present in care homes would in other circumstances be in nursing homes'.[24] The reverse, concerning the alternative placement of nursing home patients, would appear to be less valid, although other studies (for example Primrose and Capewell[25]) have indicated that many nursing home patients may be sufficiently fit to be in residential homes. However, Primrose and Capewell note that nursing homes provide the opportunity for more intensive care for patients who become older and more dependent, and the Wagner Committee recognised the importance of facilitating continuity of care in its recommendation that the registration and inspection system should be unified.[26] The importance of continuity of care between residential and nursing homes also underlies the introduction of dual registration of homes as both residential and nursing homes.[19]

With the exception of homes for people with a physical handicap, voluntary residential homes tended to accommodate people with lower levels of dependency than private residential homes. Residents in voluntary residential homes for people with a physical handicap had lower levels of mobility and more self-care problems than residents in private homes, and levels of continence, confusion and behaviour problems were more similar to those in private homes than was the case for residential homes for other client groups. There were no consistent differences in the levels of physical disability among patients in voluntary and private nursing homes, and there was little difference in the prevalence of behaviour problems, but levels of confusion were substantially lower in voluntary homes and a higher proportion of patients were fully continent. These results are summarised in the aggregate dependency classification presented in table 7. The proportions of residents and patients classified as appreciably or heavily dependent, expressed as percentages, were as follows:

Management	Resid - elderly	Resid - m. hand.	Resid - m. ill	Resid - p. hand.	Nursing homes
Voluntary	30	15	8	46	63
Private	40	26	31	33	71

Financial support of residents and patients

Approximately fifty per cent of individuals in residential homes for elderly people and nursing homes received financial support from supplementary benefit, and forty two per cent of the residents of residential homes and forty five per cent of the patients in private nursing homes were recorded as paying charges with private means. Higher proportions of individuals in the residential homes for the other client groups received financial support from supplementary benefit, and smaller proportions paid their charges with private means, particularly in homes for people with a mental handicap or a mental illness. A smaller proportion of patients in voluntary nursing homes also paid their charges by private means (twenty four per cent). Eighty six per cent of individuals in homes for people with a mental handicap received supplementary benefit (eighty five per cent in voluntary homes and eighty eight per cent in private homes), as did eighty two per cent of individuals in homes for people with a mental illness (ninety one per cent in voluntary homes and seventy eight per cent in private homes) and seventy per cent of individuals in homes for people with a physical handicap (seventy nine per cent in voluntary homes and fifty nine per cent in private homes). The greatest proportion of individuals receiving supplementary benefit topped up by other organisations or individuals occurred in private residential homes for people with a mental handicap (thirty five per cent), and in voluntary residential homes for people with a mental handicap (forty nine per cent), a mental illness (twenty eight per cent), or a physical handicap (thirty two per cent). The average age of the residents in each of these groups of homes was below pensionable age, and thus the residents would be more likely to be eligible for supplementary benefit topped up by a local authority, which is restricted to supplementary benefit recipients below pensionable age in residential homes.[27] Individuals in voluntary nursing homes (twenty three per cent) and in voluntary residential homes for people with a mental handicap (twelve per cent) were more likely to receive full financial support from a health authority or a local authority than were people in the other types of home.

Charges to residents and patients
The weekly supplementary benefit board and lodging limits (pounds per week) which came into effect in July 1986 were as follows (Minister of State for Social Security, 1986):

	Resid - elderly	Resid - m. hand.	Resid - m. ill	Resid - p. hand.	Nursing homes
London	142.50	167.50	147.50	197.50	187.50-247.50
Elsewhere	125.00	150.00	130.00	180.00	170.00-230.00

In London, mean charges to residents and patients in private homes were higher than in voluntary homes. Outside London, mean charges to individuals in private homes were only significantly higher than those in voluntary homes for residential homes for the elderly; in residential homes for people with a physical handicap the mean charges in private homes were lower than in voluntary homes. Mean charges to residents and patients were not systematically related to their source of finance, although in private residential homes and in nursing homes mean charges to individuals receiving supplementary benefit without topping up from other organisations or individuals were generally similar to the supplementary benefit board and lodging limits. However, for most types of home in London the number of homes and individuals included in the survey is too small to draw firm conclusions, and a similar problem arises for a number of financial support categories for homes outside London. Overall comparisons between the mean charges and the supplementary benefit limits on board and lodging for residential homes for people with a physical handicap and nursing homes are also complicated by the fact that several limits apply for these homes, depending on the type of resident or patient. The supplementary benefit limits for residential homes for people with a physical handicap, presented above, relate to individuals under pensionable age. The supplementary benefit limit for individuals over pensionable age in such homes was the same as for residential homes for elderly people. The private residential homes for people with a physical handicap were largely catering for elderly people, as noted above, and thus the means of 134 pounds for private homes and 172 pounds for voluntary homes outside London correspond fairly closely to the appropriate supplementary benefit limits. The mean for voluntary homes in London was 147 pounds, but this figure was based on a small number of individuals.

The mean weekly charges to individuals in private homes were slightly higher than average for people paying the charges by private means, and slightly lower than average for people supported by supplementary benefit without topping up, except for residential homes for people with a mental handicap. However, in most cases the mean charges to individuals supported by supplementary benefit with topping up were similar to those for individuals supported by private means. In voluntary homes the mean weekly charges to individuals supported by private means were generally lower than average, the exceptions to this being confined to cases based on very small number of individuals, while the mean weekly charges to individuals supported by supplementary benefit without topping up were not consistently above or below the overall mean. In voluntary residential homes for elderly people living in London, the mean weekly charge to residents supported by private means was lower than the mean charge to residents supported by supplementary benefit without topping up, whereas the mean charges to residents receiving the two types of financial support were almost identical in such homes outside London.

Comparisons of homes for elderly people over time

Introduction

The PSSRU/CHE survey was designed to be compatible with the 1981 PSSRU survey of local authority, voluntary and private residential homes for elderly people which, in turn, used questionnaires developed from those used in the 1970 Census of Residential Accommodation[6] and the (unpublished) 1971 DHSS sample survey of private residential homes. Table 8 presents information from the PSSRU/CHE survey relating to residential homes for elderly people, together with equivalent information collected in 1981 and 1970/71. Differences arise from the inclusion of homes for younger people with a physical handicap in the 1970/71 figures, and some additional differences may be expected due to sampling and response variability. It should also be noted that in the 1981 survey the voluntary homes were concentrated in a small number of the participating local authorities and may have been less representative of voluntary homes generally than the homes included in the 1986 survey, which were distributed more evenly across the selected authorities.

Characteristics of homes
Relatively limited information about the characteristics of private homes was collected in 1971 and 1981 and the comparative information about homes presented in the table is restricted to information on the average sizes of homes, whether the home had a lift, the number of storeys used by residents, and information on bedroom sizes. The information on the sizes of homes in the three sectors suggests that there have not been any dramatic changes in the average sizes of homes for elderly people during the period 1970 to 1986, although the average size of private homes may have increased slightly. A higher proportion of the voluntary and private homes for elderly people in the PSSRU/CHE survey than the homes surveyed in 1981 had a lift or a single storey for residents, and compared with 1970/71 the information collected in the two surveys indicates that a smaller proportion of residents occupied bedrooms with three or more beds in 1981 and 1986.

Characteristics of the residents
Four-fifths of the residents in homes for elderly people in the 1986 survey were female, a higher proportion than in voluntary homes in the 1970 census and the 1981 survey, and a lower proportion than in private homes in the 1971 and 1981 surveys. Information drawn from the Gazetteer of Residential accommodation, supplied to the PSSRU by the Department of Health, shows that seventy five per cent of residents in local authority and voluntary old people's homes in England in March 1986 were female, compared with eighty one per cent of residents in private homes.

The average age of residents in voluntary homes was slightly higher in 1986 than in 1981, whereas the reverse was true for private homes, mainly due to differences in the average age of male residents between the two years.

Overall, the mean lengths of stay of residents were lower in 1986 than in 1981; fifty months in voluntary homes, and twenty two months compared with twenty five months for private homes. For male residents of private homes the mean length of stay in 1986 was slightly greater than in 1981, but the difference was not statistically significant.

In 1986 residents of voluntary homes were most likely to have been living alone prior to admission (52 per cent of permanent residents). Residents of private homes were most likely either to have been living alone or to have been in hospital (33 per cent in each case). Similar distributions for the source of admission were observed in the 1981 survey, although the proportion of residents admitted from hospital was higher in 1986 than in 1981 for both voluntary and private homes.

In a previous analysis of changes in dependency between 1970/71 and 1981 based on the same data sources, it was noted that resident dependency had increased in all three sectors but changes in the voluntary sector were relatively small, while changes in the private sector were most marked.[3] A further decline in aggregate dependency in voluntary homes appears to have occurred between 1981 and 1986, in both physical and mental state (confusion), although not in relation to levels of psychological disturbance. However, aggregate levels of dependency in private homes in 1986 were very similar to those in the private homes included in the 1981 survey. Thirty per cent of residents in voluntary homes in 1986 were classified as appreciably or heavily dependent, compared with nineteen per cent in 1981, while the corresponding figures for private homes were 40 per cent (1986) and 38 per cent (1981).

The information collected in the 1981 survey indicated overall that, residents in local authority and private homes had similar levels of dependency, particularly in relation to physical abilities and continence and to a lesser extent mental state, and were much more dependent than residents in voluntary homes. However, a higher proportion of residents in private homes were relatively independent, 34 per cent being classified as minimally dependent, compared with 25 per cent of residents in local authority homes. Other recent comparative studies, including local authority and private homes, have been based on much smaller samples than the 1981 survey and have produced varying results on the relative levels of dependency in the two sectors. The studies by Wade et al.[8] in five local authorities, by Cooper[28] in one area in Essex, and by Bloomfield[29] in Coventry found generally similar levels of dependency in homes in the two sectors, whereas the studies by the Association of Directors of Social Services,[30] in ten homes from each of ten local authorities, and by Tibbenham[31] in Devon found lower levels of dependency in the private sector. As reported in table 1, the number of residents in private homes for elderly people and younger people with a physical handicap increased by 143 per cent between 1981 and 1986. During the same period the number of elderly people in England and Wales aged 75 and over increased by twelve per cent, and the number aged eighty and over increased by eighteen per cent, according to figures in the Monthly Digest of Statistics.[10] A reduction in average levels of dependency in private homes in areas of high growth such as Devon may therefore be expected, compared with areas which have experienced less growth. Essex had also experienced growth in the private sector, but the area chosen for the study had a relative shortfall in local authority beds and a high level of unsuitable local authority accommodation.

Staffing levels

Staffing ratios calculated for private and voluntary homes for 1986 were higher than those calculated for 1981, although similar amounts of time were contributed by proprietors and members of their families in the two years.

In 1981 staffing ratios for voluntary homes were lower than in local authority residential homes, while staffing ratios for private homes, including the time of proprietors and members of their families and assuming an arbitrary maximum of eighty four hours per week, were slightly higher per place, and substantially higher per resident, reflecting lower occupancy levels in private homes. The relative staffing levels are broadly consistent with the relative levels of dependency and the possible economies of scale in staffing ratios available to local authority homes. However, although the higher staffing ratios for voluntary homes in 1986 compared to 1981 may be due, at least in part, to changes in aggregate levels of dependency, in the private sector the higher staffing ratios in 1986 compared with 1981 were not accompanied by a parallel increase in dependency levels. The change in staffing levels in private homes, and possibly in voluntary sector homes as well, may be a response to the greater emphasis on registration and regulation of homes during the 1980s, particularly following the Registered Homes Act 1984.

For local authority homes in England and Wales as a whole, calculations using DHSS, Welsh Office and CIPFA statistics indicate that staffing ratios have increased very slightly from nineteen hours per place per week at the time of the 1981 PSRU survey, to twenty hours per place per week in 1986.[32,33,34,35,36] For the authorities included in the 1981 survey, the mean staffing ratios per place calculated from national statistics was also nineteen hours per place per week, compared with twenty hours per available place per week computed from the data collected from the homes in the survey.

Summary

Information collected in the 1986 PSSRU/CHE survey has provided the opportunity to compare the characteristics of residential care and nursing homes and to compare residential care homes catering for the numerically most important client groups. In addition, the survey was designed to be compatible with a survey of local authority, voluntary and private residential care homes for elderly people conducted in 1981, and was also comparable with data collected by the DHSS in 1970 and 1971.

In terms of physical characteristics residential homes for elderly people, residential homes for people with a physical handicap, and nursing homes had a higher proportion of single bedrooms than residential homes for people with a mental handicap or a mental illness and either had a lift or accommodated residents and patients on one storey. For homes catering for people with physical disabilities, voluntary homes tended to have higher standards of provision than private homes. Nursing homes had lower levels of WC provision than residential homes, but different recommended levels of provision apply to nursing homes. Compared with the information collected in 1981, a higher proportion of the residential homes for elderly people in the 1986 survey had a lift or a single storey for residents, and, at least in the private sector, fewer residents were accommodated in multiply-occupied bedrooms. In all three sectors the use of multiply-occupied bedrooms had declined substantially since 1970.

Over 80 per cent of the residents of residential homes for people with a mental handicap or a mental illness received support from supplementary benefit, compared with 70 per cent of residents in residential homes for a physical handicap and approximately 50 per cent of people in residential homes for elderly people and nursing homes. Dependency levels among patients in nursing homes were substantially higher than among residents of residential homes, particularly for physical disability and incontinence. Mental confusion was also more prevalent in nursing homes than in residential homes, while behavioural and psychological problems were more prevalent in residential homes for people with a mental handicap and in private homes for people with a mental illness. Among residential homes, residents in voluntary homes tended to be less dependent than residents in private homes, except in homes for people with a physical handicap. Among nursing homes levels of physical disability and behaviour problems were similar in both the private and voluntary sectors but levels of confusion were lower in voluntary homes and a higher proportion of patients were fully continent. Levels of dependency among residents of homes for elderly people had increased between 1970/71 and 1981, although changes in the voluntary sector were relatively small. Between 1981 and 1986 a further decline in dependency in voluntary homes appears to have occurred in physical and mental state, though not in levels of psychological disturbance, but aggregate dependency levels in private homes were very similar to those in 1981. However, the number of residents in private homes had increased by 143 per cent between 1981 and 1986, compared with an increase of twelve per cent in the number of people aged 75 five and over.

Staffing ratios in nursing homes were higher than in residential homes, but varied considerably between the various types of residential home. Including the time of proprietors and members of their families, relative staffing ratios were broadly consistent with aggregate dependency levels of residents and patients. Staffing ratios in residential homes for elderly people in 1986 were higher than in 1981 for both voluntary and private homes, although this can only be attributed partially to changes in aggregate dependency levels, and further analysis of the staffing information needs to be undertaken to examine the relationship between staffing levels, client dependency and other factors.

Appendix

Technical details of the survey

The PSSRU/CHE survey was conducted in a sample of 855 establishments in seventeen local authority areas in England, Scotland and Wales. The distribution of homes for different client groups prevented the use of a random sampling procedure for selecting authorities. Since the numbers of private residential homes for elderly people had grown in most areas of the country, such a procedure would with an appropriate stratification of areas have been satisfactory for selecting a sample of areas for a study of residential homes for elderly people. However, since homes for people in the younger client groups were more numerous in non-metropolitan areas, and recent previous research had also been undertaken in non-metropolitan areas, there was a danger of such areas becoming 'over-researched', with the consequent likelihood of lower levels of response. A purposive sampling procedure, including stratification by type of area, was employed for the selection of areas. The classification of local authorities in the DHSS summary of Local Authority Planning Statement (LAPS) returns (DHSS, 1979) was used to stratify authorities for the 1981 PSSRU survey, and the same classification was used to select areas in England and Wales for the 1986/87 survey. Scottish authorities were selected separately. Health authorities falling largely within the selected local authorities were included in the sample. The seventeen authorities selected included six English counties, four metropolitan districts, four London boroughs, one Welsh county, and two Scottish authorities. The concentration was on authorities with relatively large numbers of homes for the younger client groups in the larger cells in the cross-classification of LAPS cluster and authority type, which provided a reasonable geographical spread and included as many regional health authorities as possible and which excluded, as far as possible, areas included in other recent studies. Six of the seventeen authorities had also been included in the 1981 PSSRU survey. Within the selected authorities all residential care and nursing homes for the younger client groups were selected, and subsamples of residential and nursing homes for elderly people were selected, except that, for two of the seventeen authorities, only residential care homes for the younger client groups were selected.

A two-stage approach to the sampled homes, based on the methodology used in the 1981 PSSRU survey and the interview follow-up conducted in private homes in

1982-83, was adopted for the survey. Since the assistance of health and local authorities to co-ordinate the collection of the questionnaires from homes would not be available and evidence from recent studies suggested that a postal questionnaire on its own would not achieve a reasonable response rate, the interviewers were required to collect the postal questionnaire from each home as well as to conduct an interview. Information relating to 31st October 1986 was collected in the survey. The fieldwork for the survey was completed in March 1987, following a break in January 1987 due to bad weather.

Six hundred and six establishments responded; this total includes separate questionnaires which were received from the two separate units of one home. The overall response rate, excluding eighty five homes found to be out of the scope of the survey, was seventy nine per cent. For fifty one of the 606 establishments, partial or late information was received, and the information presented in this paper relates to 555 homes.

The classification of homes by type of home and client group for this paper is based on the information contained in the lists of homes used for selecting the sample. Residential homes caring for more than one client group were classified as follows:

- homes for elderly people and people with a mental infirmity were included with homes for elderly people;
- homes for elderly people and people with a physical handicap were included with homes for people with a physical handicap;
- and homes for other combinations of client groups were classified according to the client group that they were recorded as principally accommodating.

The method of classifying residential homes caring for more than one client group ensured that only homes caring specifically or principally for elderly people were excluded from the two authorities in which the sample was restricted to residential care homes for the younger client groups. However, further analysis of the classification of homes using information recorded on the questionnaire for homes has revealed that a number of homes would be more appropriately classified as principally accommodating another client group. Such a classification would only affect a small number of residential homes for elderly people, people with a mental handicap or a mental illness, but would affect a larger number of (mainly private) residential homes classified as catering for people with a physical handicap. Sixty seven residential homes for people with a physical handicap are included in the tables, of which thirty five were voluntary and thirty two private homes. Twenty seven of these homes, (twenty six private and one voluntary home), would be more appropriately classified as principally accommodating another client group, (twenty four for elderly people, one for people with a mental handicap and two for people with a mental illness). Thus, whereas the voluntary residential homes for people with a physical handicap were correctly classified, the majority of private residential homes for people with a physical handicap catered for elderly people. It has not been possible to reclassify homes for the purposes of this paper and the information presented in the tables for private residential homes for people with a physical handicap should be interpreted as catering largely for elderly people.

Dual registered homes which appeared on the sampling lists for both residential and nursing homes were included with residential homes, and dual registered homes which only appeared on one of the sampling lists were classified according to whether the list related to residential or nursing homes. Fifty six of the 555 homes included in the tables in this paper reported that they were registered with both a health authority and a social services department. However, the information provided by homes on the registering authority or authorities may be unreliable. Only fourteen of the fifty six homes are listed as dual registered in the directory of private healthcare published by Laing and Buisson.[37] Twelve of these homes are classified as residential homes and two are classified as nursing homes.

The computation of appropriate statistical tests for comparing differences between types of home is complicated by the complex design of the study. Statistical tests based on simple random sampling assumptions have been used to identify such differences, but will overestimate the number of statistically significant differences. Differences which do not meet the five per cent criterion of statistical significance under these assumptions are not discussed in the text.

Acknowledgments

The data discussed in this paper were collected in two projects funded by the former Department of Health and Social Security. The DHSS also made available information from the 1970 Census of Residential Accommodation, the 1971 sample survey of private homes and the 1986 Gazetteer of Residential Accommodation. Responsibility for the paper is the authors' alone. Sheila Jefferson and Eileen Sutcliffe at the University of York were responsible for organising the fieldwork and data preparation for the 1986 survey. Finally, without the cooperation of proprietors and managers of residential and nursing homes, the study would not have been possible, and their willingness to participate is gratefully acknowledged.

References

1. Ernst and Whinney. *Survey of Private and Voluntary Residential and Nursing Homes for the Department of Health and Social Security.* Ernst and Whinney, London, 1986.

2. Darton, R. A. and Knapp, M. R. J. 'The Cost of Residential Care for the Elderly: The Effects of Dependency, Design and Social Environment' *Ageing and Society*. 4, Part 2, 1984, 157-183.

3. Darton, R. A. 'Trends 1970-81.' In Laming, H. et al. *Residential Care for the Elderly: Present Problems and Future Issues*. Discussion Paper No.8. Policy Studies Institute, London, 1984.

4. Judge, K., Knapp, M. R. J. and Smith, J. 'The Comparative Costs of Public and Private Residential Homes for the Elderly.' In Judge, K. and Sinclair, I. (Eds.) *Residential Care for Elderly People*. HMSO, London, 1986.

5. Davies, B. P and Knapp, M. R. J. 'Hotel and Dependency Costs of Residents in Old People's Homes' *Journal of Social Policy*. 7, Part 1, 1978, 1-22.

6. Department of Health and Social Security. *The Census of Residential Accommodation: 1970. I. Residential Accommodation for the Elderly and for the Younger Physically Handicapped.*

7. Challis, L. with Day, P. *Private and Voluntary Residential Provision for the Elderly. Report of an Exploratory Study of Residential and Nursing homes in the City of Bath*. Centre for the Analysis of Social Policy, University of Bath.

8. Wade, B., Sawyer, L. and Bell, J. *Dependency with Dignity: Different Care Provision for the Elderly*. Occasional Papers on Social Administration No.68. Bedford Square Press, London, 1983.

9. Larder, D., Day, P. and Klein, R. *Institutional Care for the Elderly: The Geographical Distribution of the Public/Private Mix in England*. Bath Social Policy Papers No.10, Centre for the Analysis of Social Policy, University of Bath, June 1986.

10. Central Statistical Office. *Monthly Digest of Statistics*. No. 324, December 1972; No. 386, February 1978; No. 451, July 1983; No. 509, May 1988. HMSO, London.

11. Department of Health and Social Security. *Local Authority Building Note Number 2. Residential Accommodation for Elderly People*. HMSO, London, 1973.

12. Centre for Policy on Ageing. *Home Life: A Code of Practice for Residential Care. Report of a Working Party Sponsored by the Department of Health and Social Security*. Centre for Policy on Ageing, London, 1984.

13. Laing and Buisson. *Care of Elderly People: The Developing Market for Nursing and Residential Homes and Related Services in Britain. Business Opportunities and Risks in a Growth Sector*. Laing and Buisson, London, 1988.

14. Ministry of Health. *Local Authority Building Note Number 2. Residential Accommodation for Elderly People*. HMSO, London, 1962.

15. National Association of Health Authorities in England and Wales. *Registration and Inspection of Nursing Homes. A Handbook for Health Authorities*. National Association of Health Authorities in England and Wales, Birmingham, 1985.

16. National Joint Council for Local Authorities' Services (Manual Workers). *Handbook* (revised edition). 1988.

17. Weaver, T., Willcocks, D. and Kellaher, L. *The Business of Care: A Study of Private Residential Homes for Old People*. CESSA Report No.1, Centre for Environmental and Social Studies in Ageing, the Polytechnic of North London, 1985.

18. Day, P. and Larder, D. *Nursing Manpower in Private and Voluntary Nursing Homes for the Elderly*. Bath Social Policy Papers No.8. Centre for the Analysis of Social Policy, University of Bath, January 1986.

Privatisation

19. Challis, L. and Bartlett, H. *Old and Ill. Private Nursing Homes for Elderly People*. Age Concern Institute of Gerontology Research Paper No.1. Age Concern England, Mitcham, 1987.

20. Knapp, M. R. J. 'On the Determination of the Manpower Requirements of Old People's Homes' *Social Policy and Administration*. 13, 3, 1979, 219-236.

21. Katz, S., Ford, A. B., Moskowitz, R. W., Jackson, B. A. and Jaffe, M. W. 'Studies of Illness in the Aged. The Index of ADL: A Standardised Measure of Biological and Psychosocial Function' *Journal of the American Medical Association*. 185, 12, 1963, 914-919.

22. Katz, S., Downs, T. D., Cash, H. R. and Grotz, R.C. 'Progress in Development of the Index of ADL' *The Gerontologist*. 10, Part 1, 1970, 20-30.

23. Davies, B.P. and Knapp, M. J. R. 'Hotel and Dependency Costs of Residents in Old People's Homes' *Journal of Social Policy*. 7, Part 1, 1978, 1-22.

24. Social Care Association. 'Considering Wagner' *Social Work Today*. 20, 6, 6th October 1988, 43.

25. Primrose, W.R. and Capewell, A. E. 'A Survey of Registered Nursing Homes in Edinburgh' *Journal of the Royal College of General Practitioners*. 36, 284, 1986, 125-128.

26. Wagner, G. *Residential Care. A Positive Choice. Report of the Independent Review of Residential Care*. HMSO, London, 1988.

27. Department of Health and Social Security. *Public Support for Residential Care. Report of a Joint Central and Local Government Working Party* (Chairman: Mrs J. Firth). 1987.

28. Cooper, M. 'The Growth of Private Residential Care in North East Essex -Its Impact on Plans for Local Authority Provision.' Social Services Department, Essex County Council, 1985.

29. Bloomfield, J. 'A Profile of Coventry's Private Care Homes for Elderly People.' Social Services Department, Coventry City Council, 1987.

30. Association of Directors of Social Services. 'Who Goes Where? A Profile of Elderly People who have Recently been Admitted to Residential Homes.' 1985.

31. Tibbenham, A. 'Private and Local Authority Care of the Elderly in Devon. A Comparative Survey of Residents and Homes.' Social Services Department, Devon County Council. 1985.

32. Department of Health and Social Security. *Local Authority Social Services Statistics. Staff of Local Authority Social Services Departments at 30 September 1981. England*. S/F 82/1, 1982.

33. Department of Health (no date). *Residential Accommodation for Elderly and for Younger Physically Handicapped People: All Residents in Local Authority, Voluntary and Private Homes. Year Ending 31 March 1981 to Year Ending 31 March 1986. England*. RA/81-86/2.

34. Welsh Office. *(no date (a)). Residential Accommodation for the Elderly, Younger Physically Handicapped and Blind. Year ended 31st March 1981.*

35. Welsh Office (no date (b)). *Residential Accommodation for the Elderly, Younger Physically Handicapped and Blind. Year ended 31st March 1982.*

36. Chartered Institute for Public Finance and Accountancy. *Personal Social Services Statistics 1986-87 Actuals*. Chartered Institute for Public Finance and Accountancy, London, 1988.

37. Laing and Buisson. *Laing's Review of Private Healthcare 1987 and Directory of Independent Hospitals, Nursing and Residential Homes and Related Services*. Laing and Buisson, London, 1987.

Table 1: Residential homes for elderly people and people with a physical handicap in England and Wales, 1970-86

	Local authority homes		Voluntary homes		Private homes		All homes	
	Number	% chge	Number	% chge	Number	% chge	Number	% chge
Homes								
1970[3]	2338		1052		1768		5158	
1976[4]	2759	18.0	1063	1.0	1814	2.6	5636	9.3
1981[4]	2862	3.7	1161	9.2	2609	43.8	6632	17.7
1986[4]	2874	0.4	1084	-6.6	6419	146.0	10377	56.5
Places								
1970[3]	n/a		33270		22712		n/a	
1976[4]	n/a	n/a	33854	1.8	27034	19.0	n/a	n/a
1981[4]	122691	n/a	38082	12.5	40737	50.7	201510	n/a
1986[4]	123578	0.7	37248	-2.2	97594	139.6	258420	28.2
Residents 65 and over								
1970[3]	92457		23773		18264		134494	
1976[4]	105586	14.2	24515	3.1	21851	19.6	151952	13.0
1981[4]	110193	4.4	26900	9.7	32941	50.8	170034	11.9
1986[4]	108748	-1.3	26018	-3.3	81608	147.7	216374	27.3
All residents								
1970[3]	99013		28566		18921		146500	
1976[4]	112218	13.3	29545	3.4	22836	20.7	164599	12.4
1981[4]	115817	3.2	33047	11.9	34830	52.5	183694	11.6
1986[4]	113600	-1.9	31608	-4.4	84746	143.3	229954	25.2

Notes

[1] From DHSS (1974) Health and Personal Social Services Statistics for England (with Summary Tables for Great Britain), 1974, London: HMSO; DHSS(nd) Residential Accommodation for Elderly and for Younger Physically Handicapped People: All Residents in Local Authority, Voluntary and Private Homes, Year Ending 31 March 1986, England, RA/86/2; Welsh Office (nd) Residential Accommodation for the Elderly and Younger Physically Handicapped, Year Ending 31st March 1976; Welsh Office (1977) Health and Personal Social Services Statistics for Wales, No.4, 1977, Cardiff: HMSO; Welsh Office (nd) Residential Accommodation for the Elderly, Younger Physically Handicapped and Blind, Year Ended 31st March 1981; Welsh Office (1986) Residential Accommodation for the Elderly, Younger Physically Handicapped and Blind: Year Ended 31/3/86, Cardiff: Welsh Office; Welsh Office (1988) Health and Personal Social Services Statistics for Wales, No. 14, 1987, Cardiff: Welsh Office.

[2] The symbol 'n/a' is used to denote information that was not available.

[3] At 31 December.

[4] At 31 March.

Privatisation

Table 2: Residential homes for elderly people and people with a physical handicap[2] in Scotland, 1970-86

	Local authority homes		Registered homes		All homes	
	Number	% chge	Number	% chge	Number	% chge
Homes						
1970[3]	206		155		361	
1976[4]	239	16.0	196	26.5	435	20.5
1981[4]	249	4.0	194	-1.0	443	1.8
1986[4]	269	8.0	249[5]	28.4	518	16.9
Places						
1970[3]	7761		4781		12542	
1976[4]	9221	18.8	5805	21.4	15026	19.8
1981[4]	9405	2.0	5787	-0.3	15192	1.1
1986[4]	9866	4.9	6750[5]	16.6	16616	9.4
Residents						
1970[3]	7350		4371		11721	
1976[4]	8433	14.7	5047	15.5	13480	15.0
1981[4]	8845	4.9	5233	3.7	14078	4.4
1986[4]	9161	3.6	6141[5]	17.4	15302	8.7

Notes

[1] From Scottish Office (1973) Scottish Abstract of Statistics, No. 3/1973, Edinburgh: HMSO; Scottish Office (1987) Statistical Bulletin, R4/1987, Residential Accommodation 1986.
[2] There were no local authority homes for people with a physical handicap during the period.
[3] At 31 December.
[4] At 31 March.
[5] The figures for the 233 voluntary and private registered homes catering for elderly people in 1986 were as follows:

	Voluntary	Private	Total
Homes	139	94	233
Places	4478	1633	6111
Residents	4144	1431	5575

Table 3: Homes and hostels for people with a mental handicap or a mental illness in England, 1977-86^2

	Local authority homes		Voluntary homes		Private homes		All homes	
	Number	% chge	Number	% chge	Number	% chge	Number	% chge
Mentally handicapped								
Homes								
1977	560		77		77		714	
1980	787	40.5	99	28.6	93	20.8	979	37.1
1983^3	963	22.4	161	62.6	131	40.9	1255	28.2
1986	1175	22.0	284	76.4	347	164.9	1806	43.9
Places								
1977	9751		1968		1298		13017	
1980	12062	23.7	2129	8.2	1617	24.6	15808	21.4
1983	13735	13.9	3054	43.4	1992	23.2	18781	18.8
1986	15788	14.9	4693	53.7	3908	96.2	24389	29.9
Mentally ill								
Homes								
1977	319		61		33		413	
1980	441	38.2	68	11.5	54	38.9	563	36.3
1983^3	527	19.5	118	73.5	53	-1.9	698	24.0
1986	597	13.3	173	46.6	151	184.9	921	31.9
Places								
1977	3092		1268		596		4956	
1980	3724	20.4	1381	8.9	761	27.7	5866	18.4
1983	4173	12.1	1601	16.1	764	0.4	6540	11.5
1986	4470	7.1	2119	32.2	1678	119.6	8267	26.4

Notes

[1] From DHSS (nd) Homes and Hostels for Mentally Ill and Mentally Handicapped People, at 31 March 1986, England, A/F 86/11.

[2] At 31 March.

[3] Data for voluntary and private homes for 1983 (and 1981 and 1982) unreliable as a result of changing the method used to collect the data.

Table 4: Homes for people with a mental handicap or a mental illness in Scotland 1976-86[2]

	Local authority homes		Registered homes		All homes	
	Number	% chge	Number	% chge	Number	% chge
Mentally handicapped						
Homes						
1978	35		12		47	
1980	44	25.7	16	33.3	60	27.7
1983	59	34.0	21	31.3	80	33.3
1986[3]	61	3.3	33	57.1	94	17.5
Places						
1978	457		496		953	
1980	561	22.8	532	7.3	1093	14.7
1983	732	30.5	646	21.4	1378	26.1
1986[3]	865	18.2	712	10.2	1577	14.4
Residents						
1978	411		449		860	
1980	495	20.4	481	7.1	976	13.5
1983	665	34.3	569	18.3	1234	26.4
1986[3]	801	20.5	662	16.3	1463	18.6
Mentally ill						
Homes						
1978	16		1		17	
1980	27	68.8	3	-	30	76.5
1983	40	48.1	2	-	42	40.0
1986[3]	30	-25.0	4	-	34	-19.0
Places						
1978	103		7	-	110	
1980	167		42	-	209	90.0
1983	239	43.1	38	-	277	32.5
1986[3]	170	-28.9	64	-	234	-15.5
Residents						
1978	88		4	-	92	
1980	142	61.4	40	-	182	97.8
1983	206	45.1	29	-	235	29.1
1986[3]	131	-36.4	58	-	189	-19.6

Notes

[1] From Scottish Office (1981) Scottish Abstract of Statistics, No. 10/1981, Edinburgh: HMSO; Scottish Office (1987) Statistical Bulletin, R4/1987, Residential Accommodation 1986.

[2] At 31 March.

[3] Group homes with minimal social work involvement excluded from tabulations for 1984 onwards (Statistical Bulletin, R2/1985, Residential Accommodation 1984, Scottish Office (1985)).

Table 5: Registered nursing homes in England and Wales, 1982-86

Year	Institutions[2]		Beds for long-stay elderly patients[3]	
	Number	% change	Number	% change
1982	1078		19013	
1983	1172	8.7	23501	23.6
1984	1350	15.2	28377	20.7
1985	1710	26.7	35225	24.1
1986	2178	27.4	44143	25.3

Notes

[1] From information recorded on form SBH 212. Information for England tabulated in DHSS (nd) Independent Sector Hospitals, Nursing Homes and Clinics in England, 31 December 1982; DHSS (nd) Independent Sector Hospitals, Nursing Homes and Clinics in England, 31 December 1983; DHSS (1987) Private Hospitals, Homes and Clinics, 31 December 1984; DHSS (1986) Private Hospitals, Homes and Clinics, 31 December 1985; DHSS (1988) Private Hospitals, Homes and Clinics, 31 December 1986. Information for Wales supplied by the Welsh Office.

[2] Excluding institutions with operating theatres.

[3] Patients aged 65 years and over requiring long-stay (i.e. 3 months and over) nursing care.

Table 6: Characteristics of Homes and Staff by Type of Home, Client Group and Management

Type of home and client group

	Resid. - elderly	Resid. - m.hand.	Resid. - m.ill	Resid. - p. hand.	Resid. homes	Nursing homes
Number of homes						
Voluntary	66	54	20	35	175	12
Private	163	76	47	32	318	50
Home size						
Voluntary						
Mean no. of registered places	29.9	18.4	19.4	34.1	26.0	38.3
Mean no. of places available	29.2	17.1	16.4	32.2	24.6	36.3
Mean no. of persons at 31/10/86	27.2	15.9	14.1	28.9	22.6	34.8
Private						
Mean no. of registered places	17.6	17.8	16.0	19.5	17.6	25.5
Mean no. of places available	17.0	15.9	15.3	18.8	16.7	25.7
Mean no. of persons at 31/10/86	15.5	14.1	14.2	16.4	15.1	23.9

	Resid. - elderly	Resid. - m.hand.	Resid. - m.ill	Resid. - p. hand.	Resid. homes	Nursing homes
Occupancy (%) of places available)						
Voluntary						
Mean	93	89	85	88	90	94
Median	96	99	87	96	96	99
Private						
Mean	89	88	93	87	89	93
Median	96	100	100	94	100	96
Year started managing home (%)						
Voluntary						
Before1971	63	12	47	71	47	80
1971 to 1980	25	33	42	15	27	20
1981 to 1983	2	33	5	6	13	0
1984 to 1986/87	10	23	5	9	13	0
Private						
Before 1971	6	11	6	0	6	14
1971 to 1980	17	20	30	17	20	27
1981 to 1983	34	20	26	20	28	28
1984 to 1986/87	43	49	38	63	46	31
Lift & no. of storeys (%)						
Voluntary						
Lift available	84	9	0	69	48	64
No lift, 1 storey	5	11	0	20	9	36
No lift, 1 storey	11	80	100	11	43	0
Private						
Lift available	61	8	17	59	42	62
No lift, 1 storey	7	5	15	0	7	0
No lift, 1 storey	32	87	67	41	51	38
Bedroom sizes (% of beds)						
Voluntary						
Single	57	37	32	51	49	56
Double	27	47	45	31	34	19
3 beds	8	10	17	6	9	8
4 beds	5	2	6	5	4	10
5 or more beds	3	4	0	7	4	7
Private						
Single	41	27	29	39	36	42
Double	46	48	48	45	46	33
3 beds	11	18	21	13	14	12
4 beds	2	6	< 1	3	3	9
5 or more beds	< 1	2	< 1	0	< 1	4
Bedrooms & building note standards[2] (%)						
Voluntary						
Meets 1973 BNS	34	13	15	27	24	18

	Resid. - elderly	Resid. - m.hand.	Resid. - m.ill	Resid. - p. hand.	Resid. homes	Nursing homes
Meets 1962 BNS						
only	26	20	20	21	22	27
Below both BNS	40	67	65	52	54	55
Private						
Meets 1973 BNS	10	5	2	6	8	8
Meets 1962 BNS						
only	29	16	21	38	26	28
Below both BNS	60	79	77	56	67	64
Mean bed:WC ratio						
Voluntary	2.9	2.8	3.6	3.1	3.0	3.6
Private	3.3	3.6	3.4	3.1	3.4	3.7
Bed:WC & building note standards[2] (%)						
Voluntary						
Meets 1973 BNS	87	89	80	88	87	67
Meets 1962 BNS						
only	13	9	20	12	12	25
Below both BNS	0	2	0	0	< 1	8
Private						
Meets 1973 BNS	80	75	83	84	80	65
Meets 1962 BNS						
only	19	21	13	13	18	27
Below both BNS	< 1	4	4	3	2	8
Mean bed:bathroom ratio						
Voluntary	6.2	4.1	5.9	7.2	5.7	6.6
Private	6.0	5.9	5.7	6.3	6.0	5.8
Common room provision (%)						
Voluntary						
No common room	0	0	5	3	1	8
One common room	23	33	5	17	23	33
More than 1						
common room	77	67	90	80	76	58
Private						
No common room	0	0	0	0	0	4
One common room	45	19	30	38	36	54
More than 1						
common room	55	81	70	63	64	42
Dining room provision (%)						
Voluntary						
No dining room	2	9	5	6	5	17
One dining room	91	69	85	71	79	83
More than 1						
dining room	8	22	10	23	16	0
Private						
No dining room	9	4	7	3	7	44

	Resid. - elderly	Resid. - m.hand.	Resid. - m.ill	Resid. - p. hand.	Resid. homes	Nursing homes
One dining room	83	84	80	84	83	52
More than 1 dining room	9	12	13	13	11	4

Distribution of no. of home staff (%)

Voluntary

Qualified nurses	10	5	13	8	9	17
Qualified care staff	3	4	11	3	4	0
Unqualified nursing & care staff	38	43	15	36	37	40
Ancillary staff	29	17	14	24	24	21
Professional & technical staff	<1	6	6	3	2	4
Admin. & clerical staff	3	6	5	5	4	3
MSC, YTS etc.	1	2	0	1	1	<1
Volunteers	3	5	5	3	4	7
Other staff	12	12	30	18	15	7

Private

Proprietors	11	17	18	13	13	5
Qualified nurses	10	5	6	11	9	27
Qualified care staff	7	5	6	4	6	
Unqualified nursing & care staff	42	38	42	49	42	39
Ancillary staff	15	15	16	14	15	18
Professional & technical staff	<1	5	1	<1	1	2
Admin. & clerical staff	1	2	3	2	2	3
MSC, YTS etc.	2	1	2	2	2	<1
Volunteers	1	3	<1	<1	2	<1
Other staff	11	10	7	4	9	4

Distribution of wte[3] home staff (%)

Voluntary

Qualified nurses	14	8	20	9	12	25
Qualified care staff	4	5	19	3	5	0
Unqualified nursing & care staff	46	55	24	46	47	42
Ancillary staff	30	17	15	28	26	22
Professional & technical staff	<1	5	5	3	2	2
Admin. & clerical staff	3	5	5	6	4	5
MSC, YTS etc.	1	2	0	2	1	<1
Volunteers	<1	1	5	<1	<1	1
Other staff	<1	1	5	2	2	1

Private

Proprietors	19	23	27	21	21	10
Qualified nurses	10	5	6	11	9	24

	Resid. - elderly	Resid. - m.hand.	Resid. - m.ill	Resid. - p. hand.	Resid. homes	Nursing homes
Qualified care staff	8	8	8	4	8	<1
Unqualified nursing & care staff	45	41	41	49	44	41
Ancillary staff	13	14	13	11	13	18
Professional & technical staff	<1	4	<1	<1	<1	<1
Admin. & clerical staff	1	2	2	<1	1	4
MSC, YTS etc.	2	<1	2	3	2	1
Voluntary	<1	1	<1	<1	<1	<1
Other	<1	<1	<1	<1	<1	<1

Staffing ratios[4] (%)

Voluntary

Employees: places available	21	27	15	32	24	37
Employees: residents/ patients	23	31	18	34	26	41

Private

Employees: places available	23	19	16	18	21	34
Employees: residents/ patients	26	21	17	22	23	37
All staff: places available	31	30	26	24	29	39
All staff: residents/ patients	35	34	28	31	33	43

Notes

[1] Percentages are rounded to whole numbers and may not sum to 100 due to rounding. The symbol '' is used to denote non-zero percentages of under one per cent.

[2] Department of Health and Social Security (1973) Local Authority Building Note Number 2: Residential Accommodation for Elderly People, London: HMSO; Ministry of Health (1962) Local Authority Building Note Number 2: Residential Accommodation for Elderly People, London: HMSO.

[3] One whole time equivalent (wte) defined as 39 hours per week to correspond to the normal working week in local authority residential homes. (The standard working week for NHS nurses is 37.5 hours per week). Hours in excess of 84 hours per week truncated to 84 hours for the purpose of calculating whole time equivalents.

[4] Hours in excess of 84 hours per week truncated to 84 hours.

Privatisation

Table 7: Characteristics of Residents/Patients by Type of Home, Client Group and Management

Type of home and client group

	Resid. - elderly	Resid. - m. hand.	Resid. - m. ill	Resid. - p. hand.	Resid. homes	Nursing homes
Number of individuals						
Voluntary	1756	855	292	936	3839	351
Private	2414	1149	666	555	4784	1150
Sex distribution (%)						
Voluntary						
Males	19	52	61	53	38	30
Females	81	48	39	47	62	70
Private						
Males	21	54	40	31	33	16
Females	79	46	60	69	67	84
Mean age						
Voluntary						
Males	81.4	34.5	41.4	54.0	52.9	65.9
Females	83.9	37.4	47.8	60.7	70.0	76.9
Males and females	83.4	35.9	43.9	57.1	63.6	73.9
Private						
Males	78.8	42.2	59.0	71.6	60.5	75.7
Females	83.3	50.4	70.0	79.1	75.9	83.6
Males and females	82.3	46.0	65.6	76.8	70.9	82.4
Mean length of stay (months)						
Voluntary						
Males	42	111	31	96	80	61
Females	51	110	60	97	71	50
Males and females	50	110	42	97	74	53
Private						
Males	20	48	41	26	35	19
Females	23	63	40	22	31	26
Males and females	22	55	41	23	33	25
Sources of admission (%)						
Voluntary						
Another home	8	38	13	23	19	20
Hospital	13	18	60	18	19	26
Living alone	52	5	5	15	29	30
Living with others	16	38	14	40	26	21
Sheltered housing	3	< 1	2	1	2	2
Hotel etc.	2	< 1	5	< 1	2	< 1
Not known	6	< 1	0	2	4	< 1
Private						
Another home	14	30	16	21	19	17

	Resid. - elderly	Resid. - m.hand.	Resid. - m.ill	Resid. - p. hand.	Resid. homes	Nursing homes
Hospital	33	41	60	38	39	45
Living alone	33	4	6	21	21	19
Living with others	15	18	8	14	14	14
Sheltered housing	2	2	1	2	2	2
Hotel etc.	<1	3	5	1	2	-1
Not known	2	1	4	2	2	2

Mobility (%)

Voluntary

Walk outdoors	46	89	97	27	55	10
Walk indoors, incl stairs	8	6	1	5	6	9
Walk indoors on level	8	1	<1	8	6	15
Walk indoors with aids	23	<1	1	15	14	15
Walk indoors with help	6	<1	0	4	4	7
Mobile in wheelchair	6	2	0	33	11	21
Chair or bedfast	3	<1	0	8	3	22

Private

Walk outdoors	36	78	67	46	52	14
Walk indoors, incl stairs	10	7	7	11	9	8
Walk indoors on level	9	4	6	7	7	8
Walk indoors with aids	23	3	10	20	16	18
Walk indoors with help	12	3	6	8	9	20
Mobile in wheelchair	6	2	3	7	5	11
Chair or bedfast	4	2	1	2	3	22

No. self-care tasks assisted[2] (%)

Voluntary

Assisted with no tasks	40	84	98	40	54	21
Assisted with 1 task	35	7	1	23	23	22
Assisted with 2 tasks	6	4	<1	4	5	8
Assisted with 3 tasks	5	3	<1	5	4	7
Assisted with 4 tasks	5	<1	0	8	5	11
Assisted with 5 tasks	5	<1	0	8	4	7
Assisted with 6 tasks	4	<1	0	11	5	23

Private

Assisted with no tasks	32	65	56	48	45	14
Assisted with 1 task	32	16	26	24	27	21
Assisted with 2 tasks	8	5	4	6	6	8
Assisted with 3 tasks	7	4	4	3	6	8
Assisted with 4 tasks	8	1	4	7	6	16

	Resid. - elderly	Resid. - m.hand.	Resid. - m.ill	Resid. - p. hand.	Resid. homes	Nursing homes
Assisted with 5 tasks	8	2	3	8	6	18
Assisted with 6 tasks	5	6	2	4	4	15
Continence (%)						
Voluntary						
Continent	72	85	93	69	76	51
Isolated incontinence	12	10	5	14	12	10
Urine incontinence	7	2	1	6	5	10
Faecal/double incontinence	9	2	0	11	7	30
Private						
Continent	61	71	71	67	65	40
Isolated incontinence	20	18	17	17	19	21
Urine incontinence	10	3	6	8	8	13
Faecal/double incontinence	9	8	5	8	8	26
Confusion (%)						
Voluntary						
Mentally alert	63	66	76	69	66	57
Mildly confused	25	22	17	23	23	29
Severely confused	12	12	7	8	10	14
Private						
Mentally alert	49	43	42	61	48	36
Mildly confused	35	41	36	27	36	39
Severely confused	17	17	21	12	17	25
Anti-social behaviour (%)						
Voluntary						
Not disruptive	88	76	85	80	83	78
Mildly disruptive	10	19	12	16	14	16
Disruptive	2	6	2	3	3	5
Private						
Not disruptive	77	55	64	77	70	74
Mildly disruptive	18	34	28	17	23	20
Disruptive	5	11	8	6	7	6
Anxiety						
Voluntary						
No evidence	60	55	49	57	58	54
Worries	26	33	35	33	30	28
Often apprehensive	7	6	12	4	7	8
Frequently tense	7	5	5	6	6	11
Private						
No evidence	52	48	34	55	49	52
Worries	32	36	34	34	33	29
Often apprehensive	9	6	15	4	9	9

	Resid. - elderly	Resid. - m.hand.	Resid. - m.ill	Resid. - p. hand.	Resid. homes	Nursing homes
Frequently tense	7	10	16	6	9	10

Depression
Voluntary

No evidence	72	76	67	71	72	65
Sadness	19	17	25	20	19	23
Sadness and weeping	5	5	5	7	5	5
Depression and guilt	4	2	3	2	3	7

Private

No evidence	67	68	51	72	66	62
Sadness	22	21	30	22	23	25
Sadness and weeping	8	8	10	4	8	9
Depression and guilt	3	4	9	1	4	4

Attitude to help (%)
Voluntary

Independent	81	86	87	75	81	66
Dependent	19	14	13	25	19	34

Private

Independent	73	71	72	78	73	57
Dependent	27	29	28	22	27	43

Index of ADL (Katz et al[3]) (%)
Voluntary

A (No dependent functions)	39	82	97	39	53	18
B (1)	34	9	2	23	24	24
C (2)	7	5	0	5	6	8
D (3)	4	<1	1	2	3	5
E (4)	4	<1	0	9	4	4
F (5)	6	<1	0	10	5	14
G (6)	4	<1	0	6	3	19
Other (2-5, not C-F)	3	<1	0	4	3	7

Private

A (no dependent functions)	30	64	55	45	44	13
B (1)	32	18	26	27	27	20
C (2)	10	6	7	6	8	8
D (3)	5	2	2	3	4	6
E (4)	8	1	3	8	6	13
F (5)	7	4	2	5	5	19
G (6)	4	4	2	2	3	14
Other (2-5, not C-F)	4	<1	2	3	3	6

DHSS 4-category dependency[4] (%)
Voluntary

Minimal	46	79	91	34	53	17
Limited	24	6	1	20	18	20
Appreciable	9	1	<1	15	8	13

	Resid. - elderly	Resid. - m.hand.	Resid. - m.ill	Resid. - p. hand.	Resid. homes	Nursing homes
Heavy	21	14	7	31	21	51
Private						
Minimal	33	64	50	45	44	13
Limited	26	11	18	22	21	17
Appreciable	11	2	6	8	8	14
Heavy	29	24	25	26	27	57
Financial support (%)						
Voluntary						
Private means	42	4	7	16	24	24
SB Board and Lodging	36	35	63	45	40	25
SB B & L, topped up	12	49	28	32	26	24
Registering LA or HA	8	6	0	4	6	19
Another LA or HA	2	6	3	3	3	4
No fees	<1	0	0	0	<1	3
Private						
Private means	42	4	13	32	27	45
SB Board and Lodging	39	53	72	42	48	28
SB B & L, topped up	12	35	6	17	17	18
Registering LA or HA	6	5	7	8	6	6
Another LA or HA	<1	3	<1	1	2	3
No fees	<1	<1	0	0	<1	<1
Mean weekly charge						
Voluntary						
London	130	113	144	166	137	188
Outside London	119	171	130	168	147	189
Private						
London	163	168	-	193	164	220
Outside London	138	176	133	139	147	197
Mean charge - London						
Voluntary						
Private means	118	-	138	148	124	209
SB Board and Lodging	140	112	137	147	137	177
SB B & L, topped up	118	122	161	219	167	180
Private						
Private means	169	168	-	197	171	233
SB Board and Lodging	150	168	-	-	152	211

	Resid. - elderly	Resid. - m.hand.	Resid. - m.ill	Resid. - p. hand.	Resid. homes	Nursing homes
SB B & L, topped up	164	169	-	142	165	225
Mean charge - outside London						
Voluntary						
Private means	111	147	188	118	116	178
SB Board and Lodging	109	127	116	172	131	199
SB B & L, topped up	136	192	145	180	175	200
Private						
Private means	143	138	141	147	143	207
SB Board and Lodging	133	144	131	134	136	184
SB B & L, topped up	141	223	147	148	183	181

Notes

[1] Percentages are rounded to whole numbers and may not sum to 100 due to rounding. The symbol '' is used to denote non-zero percentages of under one per cent.
[2] The self-care tasks included are: washing face and hands, bathing, dressing, feeding self, using the WC, and transferring from bed/chair.
[3] Katz, S. et al. (1963) Studies of Illness in the Aged. The Index of ADL: A Standardized Measure of Biological and Psychosocial Function, Journal of the American Medical Association, 185, No.12, 914-919; Katz, S. et al. (1970) Progress in the Development of the Index of ADL, The Gerontologist, 10, Part 1, 20-30.
[4] Davies, B.P. and Knapp, M.R.J. (1978) Hotel and Dependency Costs of Residents of Old People's Homes, Journal of Social Policy, 7, Part 1, 1-22.

Table 8: Characteristics of Residential Homes for Elderly People, 1970-86, by Type of Management

	Local authority homes		Voluntary homes			Private homes		
	1970	1981	1970	1981	1986	1971	1981	1986
Number of homes[3]	2392	235	1073	68	66	362	153	163
Mean no. of places available	46	46	31	27	29	13	15	17
Lift & No. of storeys (%)								
Lift available	n/a	74	n/a	68	84	n/a	27	61
No lift, 1 storey	n/a	15	n/a	3	5	n/a	12	7
No lift, 1 storey	n/a	10	n/a	29	11	n/a	61	32
Distribution of beds (%)								
Single bedrooms	30	53	46	72	57	35	41	41
Double bedrooms	30	32	20	16	27	35	29	46
3 + bedded rooms	40	15	34	12	15	30	30	14
Sex distribution of residents (%)								
Males	33	27	29	30	19	14	14	21

	Local authority homes		Voluntary homes			Private homes		
	1970	1981	1970	1981	1986	1971	1981	1986
Females	67	73	71	70	81	86	86	79
Mean age of residents								
Males	n/a	79.0	n/a	78.1	81.4	n/a	81.2	78.8
Females	n/a	83.3	n/a	83.7	83.9	n/a	84.2	83.3
Males and females	n/a	82.1	n/a	82.1	83.4	n/a	83.8	82.3
Mean length of stay (months)								
Males	n/a	38	n/a	52	42	n/a	18	20
Females	n/a	38	n/a	58	51	n/a	26	23
Males and females	n/a	38	n/a	57	50	n/a	25	22
Sources of admission of permanent residents (%)								
Another home	19	12	10	9	8	n/a	17	14
Hospital	30	35	13	8	13	n/a	26	33
Living alone	24	29	34	47	52	n/a	33	33
Living with others	21	17	30	16	16	n/a	17	14
Sheltered housing	2	4	3	6	3	n/a	1	3
Other/not known	5	3	11	13	9	n/a	6	3
Mobility (%)								
Walk outdoors	} 49	30	} 63	50	46	} 70	31	36
Walk indoors, incl. stairs		7		9	8		12	10
Walk indoors on level	7	13	6	8	8	14	8	9
Walk indoors with aids	29	34	16	22	23	} 12	25	23
Walk indoors with help	9	9	5	6	6		13	12
Mobile in wheelchair	5	7	8	4	6	2	7	6
Chair or bedfast	1	<1	3	<1	3	2	3	4
Continence (%)								
Continent	71	60	84	83	72	81	59	61
Isolated incontinence	15	19	9	9	12	10	21	20
Urine incontinence	7	10	4	5	7	5	9	10
Faecal/double incontinence	6	11	3	3	9	4	11	9
Confusion (%)								
Mentally alert	56	45	77	72	63	74	50	49
Mildly confused	32	37	19	21	25	22	36	35
Severely confused	12	19	4	7	12	4	14	17
DHSS 4-category dependency (%)								
Minimal	30	25	63	59	46	n/a	34	33
Limited	40	36	20	22	24	n/a	29	26
Appreciable	11	11	5	7	9	n/a	10	11
Heavy	19	28	12	12	21	n/a	28	29

	Local authority homes		Voluntary homes			Private homes		
	1970	1981	1970	1981	1986	1971	1981	1986
Staffing ratios[4] (hours per week)								
Employees: places available	n/a	20	n/a	15	21	n/a	14	23
Employees: residents/patients	15	21.	15	16	23	n/a	17	26
All staff: places available	n/a	20	n/a	15	21	n/a	22	31
All staff: residents/places	15	21	15	16	23	n/a	27	35

Notes

1. Percentages are rounded to whole numbers and may not sum to 100 due to rounding. The symbol '' is used to denote non-zero percentages of under one per cent.
2. The symbol 'n/a' is used to denote information that was not available.
3. Distribution of beds and DHSS 4-category dependency for 1970 based on 188 local authority homes and 81 voluntary homes in the local authority areas surveyed in 1981
4. Hours in excess of 84 hours per week truncated to 84 hours.

Public and Private Residential Care for Elderly People: The Social Work Task

Judith Phillips and Peter McCoy

Introduction

The current media attention focusing on public/private residential care is an excellent example of the way that we learn nothing from history, except as proof that we learn nothing from history. Not only has private residential provision for elderly people co-existed with public provision for at least a century, but the rhetoric about care regimes in private homes has changed very little, as the following quotes from homes' advertising literature show:

'provides a good environment for people who wish to spend their retirement years in comfort and security in a caring family atmosphere ... All medical treatments normally dealt with by trained nursing staff ... Regular visits are undertaken by the home's medical officer ... Special emphasis is placed on individual happiness.'

'conducted on the plan of a private family; freedom from bodily restraints, accompanied with kindness and liberality of treatment; also, the advantage of the best medical attendance.'

The first is from a brochure for a private home sent out in 1988, the second from a handbill for Cheek Point House Private Lunatic Asylum, County Waterford, Southern Ireland, June 1852. There are of course differences - Cheek Point probably did not have a Century medi whirlpool bath - but the assumptions about the public role of private care as an accepted fact of provision are the same. So why has there been all the recent fuss?

This is, of course, a rhetorical question. Yet to show the parallel between the professions of good intentions outlined above, it is clear that bad practice existed in the past, and continues to the present, as evidenced by the various outcries about specific private AND public homes: it can also be argued that such media managed events are just the tip of the iceberg, or that they are highly atypical. Who knows which view is more accurate or how it could be measured empirically? In the current climate of reborn certainties, who is going to fund the next 'Last Refuge' type study, and would it have any effect if done? Has social care policy become the exclusive domain of public relations or political rhetoric to the exclusion of research or policy related practice? Hence, perhaps, the fuss.

A major point for researchers and would-be policy makers to note is that the dilemma posed by the co-existence of public and private care is not new. The basic practice and policy options were clearly laid out in 'The Last Refuge', but private care was not then a live issue and there was very little reaction to the findings of that part of the study.[1] While private care only became a political issue in the 1980s, it had, unnoticed, been growing faster than the public sector since the 1960s.[2] When it became a topic for research, the focus was on the arithmetic of its growth,[3] on the type of residents that it cares for,[4] and on the expanding and changing roles for Local Authority Registration Officers.[5]

There has been almost no research work into how this major change in provision affects social work practice. The traditional roles of social workers, at field work and management level, have been to assess professionally whether residential care is needed, and subsequently to arrange for a place in a part III home. Given the changes of the last twenty years, both in inter-sectoral levels of provision and in broader public perceptions of who does what, is this still a valid role for agency workers to pursue? If not, what role, if any, does a social worker have in the process of admission to private residential care, and whose is the decision?

The research context

A three year ESRC funded research study looking at the critical steps in the journey into care and the various processes operating in an admission was undertaken between 1985 and 1988. Two hundred elderly people who in one year entered thirty nine private homes in Suffolk were interviewed in relation to their process of admission. A series of interviews were also conducted with relatives and significant professionals involved in the journey into care. Forty two social workers were contacted by telephone and asked to describe their role, the extent of their involvement and attitude toward the private sector.

A comparative study of 120 elderly people entering local authority homes also took place, involving interviews with thirty eight different social workers on similar themes.

Research findings

Social worker participation in the process

The issues mentioned earlier raise questions of social worker participation in the processes of private care. There were several reasons why social workers were reluctant to work in the private sector or even to entertain thoughts of working on the fringe of this alternative sector by helping admissions to private homes. The stereotype of a 'left wing' social worker holding anti-privatisation views may provide one reason for their reluctance to become involved, but other reasons are more apparent. There was a lack of knowledge and training, not only about the private sector as a whole, but also about the characteristics of private sector homes. There was mutual suspicion between social workers and proprietors which did not foster an enthusiastic working relationship: social workers saw that the proprietors' primary purpose was to make a profit and felt that this was incompatible with good quality care; proprietors were sceptical about the genuineness of social workers' assessments and saw their goal as merely wanting to get the elderly person settled in somewhere.

Despite this, of the 200 people admitted to Private Residential Care, eighty nine (forty four per cent) had some contact with a social worker. However, the level of involvement varied considerably, and can be categorised as follows.

A Twenty four (twelve per cent) of these elderly people went through the process of admission with the social worker playing a significant part throughout - i.e. through the admission, decision-making, negotiation with placement owners on the client's behalf, enabling the client to get through the transition period and through the practicalities of the admission itself.

B Fifteen (eight per cent) were assessed as needing residential care and given some help.

C Fourteen (seven per cent) were recommended to a private home with no follow up given.

D Eighteen (nine per cent) were given only a marginal service (they were given a list of homes).

E Eighteen (nine per cent) social workers withdrew on the grounds that admission to private residential care was not an appropriate task.

There was considerable participation on the part of social workers, far more than was given by community health staff (GP/DN/HV/CPNs were involved in thirty one cases). Only twenty one of the residents had acted as 'independent consumers' buying directly into private residential care without using professional or other mediation. Professional participation was very varied.

Circumstances in which social workers became involved in the admission to private care

A pragmatic response

Working within the public sector, eighteen of the forty two social workers interviewed in the study of admissions to private care expressed mixed feelings about their role, considering themselves forced into accepting this position through lack of resources within their own sector of operation. They viewed themselves first and foremost as gatekeepers to the Local Authority system, but, faced by a lack of available beds and a long waiting list, they turned to the private sector for a quick solution. This resulted in five per cent of elderly people entering private care.

SW 'We are forced to use the private sector a lot. In principle we don't like it but when people can't go home from hospital and have to await a Part III vacancy then it's often a case of having to look to the private sector, particularly if it is for a married couple.'

Social workers such as this felt their relationship with home owners was based on necessity - that it was artificial but necessary as a result of the lack of appropriate alternative resources.

In the best interests of the elderly person

Social workers were involved with eight per cent of admissions to meet the needs of the elderly people in the most appropriate way. There was no preference for one sector of care over the other: the home chosen was seen as being the most appropriate response, because what the home provided matched the needs of the elderly person - e.g. a private home offered ramps for wheelchair access, specialised bathroom facilities for disabled people, or was seen to be meeting the needs of a wheelchair user.

Advocates for elderly people with no family

Where no family were involved social workers (fifteen out of forty two) were becoming involved as advocates on the elderly person's behalf, as people able or given the authority to act on behalf of the elderly person in negotiation with the home owner and often to become the arbiter between other professionals, for example, between GPs and housing authorities.

Local knowledge of local homes

It was apparent that many residents of some homes had been channeled by social workers into a particular home. In discussion with the social workers, some saw themselves in the role of investigating the 'good' while boycotting the 'bad' and fostering a working relationship with homes. This was particularly true for hospital social workers who had worked for a number of years in admissions of numerous elderly people, building up a network of contacts which could be tapped when needed. Such networks were established particularly between social workers covering psychogeriatric wards and home owners taking people suffering from senile dementia: an established channel of communication existed. The social workers had several clients in a home and would visit them. There were very few such homes and it was possible for the social worker to get to know them in some depth.

Political preference

Although only eighteen elderly people were placed in private care by social workers with a political bias toward the private sector, nearly half the social workers interviewed expressed such a preference: these social workers were predominantly in hospital social work (sixteen out of eighteen).

SW 'I prefer to use the private sector, it suits my politics.'

These social workers can be balanced against those with different preferences.

SW 'I don't want to deal with the private sector. Personally I disapprove. It doesn't offer safeguards, consistency, protection or security, just profit.'

In some instances (four per cent of admissions) social workers saw their role as functioning in the public sector alone and withdrew their involvement when they were faced with a *lack of public sector resources* to offer. They did not see their role as extending to the private sector even when resources in the public sector were not available.

Two social workers felt they should not be involved in the private sector if relatives were available to help the elderly person. Intruding into a private arrangement between families and home owners was not seen as a legitimate role for them.

SW 'If the family are keen on private care after I've explained the options, then they can go away and explore it themselves. We tell them about it but it is a private arrangement.'

Other factors relevant to involvement

Seven families chose to ignore the social worker in the process because they could not perceive the social worker in a helpful role, particularly if there were no vacancies in Part III homes.

SW 'I was involved in discussing future plans and I assessed her [elderly person] for different options, but they didn't look at any homes with me as the daughter presented it to me *fait accompli* - they had found a vacancy.'

Other professionals, particularly in the health service, bypassed social workers in four per cent of admissions of elderly people, again because they saw their role as one existing purely within the public sector.

What this shows is that some social workers were actively using their skills outside the realms of the public sector and taking on a variety of roles - both traditional roles of assessment and new roles as consultants/inspectors to private sector homes. Others did not and a number of reasons were given. However, their overall level of participation was very varied and in many cases was marginal in relation to that of other key operators, the primary carers and heads of private homes. While forty four per cent of the residents had contacted a social worker, only twelve per cent enjoyed a full social work service throughout the process of admission. The variability of social worker's involvement led to elderly people receiving an unequal service: some social workers, by operating within their personal preferences and withdrawing their involvement, acted as barriers and deprived elderly people of an informed choice. Elderly people and their families received conflicting messages from the same agency.

Thus the move into the market system was not encouraged in any planned, systematic way nor governed by policy initiatives, and as a result some social workers acted autonomously; social workers acted outside defined agency functions, though the agency at that time did not define closely social workers' roles and functions in relation to the private sector. In contrast social services departments responded to their legislative function of registration by actively promoting an ethos of pluralism, developing ways of maximising the potential of private and voluntary provision as well as that of the Local Authority. In the registration sphere, private care was 'not seen as the opposite end of the welfare spectrum to Local Authority provision.'

Implications for practice

The data clearly show that the number of people in private residential care is rising continuously, though perhaps not at the same pace as in the early 1980s. Whether this recent retrenchment in Suffolk is due to Government concern about the sums resulting from this policy or to potential home owners facing escalating house prices is debatable. But the issues raised in this research are not going to go away.

It is difficult to examine the implications of this research for future practice given the delayed implementation of the Griffiths and other reports, but a number of general points are clear.

Agencies' policy

The assessment of need has never been the present government's highest priority, although at one level it has been argued that:

'...the blind, unplanned, unco-ordinated wisdom of the market is overwhelmingly superior to the well-researched, rational, systematic, well-meaning, co-operative, science-based, forward-looking, statistically respectable plans of governments, bureaucracies and international organisations preserved from human error and made thoroughly respectable by the employment of numerous computers'.[6]

The escalation of costs of public support for residential care raises many questions.

BASW has produced practice notes which stress the social work role as 'an independent voice on behalf of the client' and emphasises 'enabling the client as far as possible to make a personal decision which might be different from that made by relatives and friends', but such a role did not feature largely in the practice as described here and BASW's policy was not well known.

There was very little evidence of social services department policy at the time of data collection. There was no translation of the declared agency policy of pluralism into practice guidelines for social workers in this area of work. Few social workers knew the agency line of pluralism, and where they did there was a lack of consistency in the social workers' knowledge of what agency policy was in terms of the private sector: half believed there existed an unspoken agreement that social workers should not place elderly people in private homes, and the other half supported the agency line on pluralism as they saw fit by promoting and participating in both sectors of care.

It is significant that pro-private sector workers were predominantly based in hospital teams, where different pressures can apply to those in community based teams. Within the department, two sets of workers are involved in private care - social workers and registration officers - and at the time of research these two were located at different levels in the organisation, the former decentralised, the latter at headquarters.

Nor were the alternatives to residential care - private or public - pursued with the vigour of some authorities, as, for example, the Kent Community Care Scheme, whereby social workers have a budget to manage which enables elderly people to stay out of residential care. A workable and working agency policy is no easy matter, but there does not appear to have been one planned at the time of the research.

In the Firth report there is an argument for tighter regulation of funding for those seeking state support. Such a recommendation may provide either an opportunity for a more comprehensive agency policy for private care, one that links social workers, registration staff, and managers of public residential and community facilities within an overall balance of care model, or for the creation of another set of discrete workers, providing a financial rationing service.

The role of social work for elderly people in the 1990s

But perhaps more important than the agency implications are the implications for social work practice. Focussing on elderly people and their needs, rather on the requirements of local or central government for efficiency and savings or accountability and control, it would seem necessary to take an overall view of provision rather than one that concentrates on one segment - private residential care.

The BASW document does seem to provide one sound starting point - enabling the elderly person to make a personal choice - and is based on recognising the conflicting pressures that impinge on some (though not all) elderly people - pressure from relatives, local and central government policies, etc. Given that the research shows that many admissions proceed without social work contact, the role of 'an independent voice' on behalf of the elderly person may well attract more customers, especially if one clear block is the 'old' social work role as perceived by Health Services staff.

However such a role is very different from that currently played. For a start, only forty eight per cent of those residents receiving DHSS funding had received help from social workers. To increase this number to cover all such applicants, as implied by Griffiths, and to make the service available to all other persons thinking about residential care, would be a sizeable expansion.

Such workers would need to expand their knowledge of local homes considerably. Not only are criteria different in private homes, but the range of services offered is wider than in local authority homes. However the research does show that to some extent some workers are already doing this. Some social workers are using those homes they see as good and avoiding those they see as bad. Many already have a good rapport with such homes, working for the benefit of their clients. They knew certain homes could cope, and that if there were any difficulties, the home owner would contact the social worker. How would this organisation deal with new homes, known to Registration Officers but not necessarily to social workers?

Finally, some social workers will have to address their own value systems and political beliefs as well as their perceptions of private residential homes. Although only four per cent of admissions involved a social worker withdrawing for 'public sector agent' or political reasons, this figure may be an underestimation as some other people may have been put off private care. In a comparative sample of social workers admitting elderly people to Local Authority residential care, higher numbers expressed opposition to the private sector.

Since the majority of elderly people did not request social work help it is difficult to get a complete picture. It would appear that social workers have to compromise their personal values because of the 'urgency' of finding a residential placement. The research shows that, although the four per cent may be an underestimation, the stereotype of social workers restricting involvement in private care provision is something of a myth. The majority worked within the system, not seeing it as outside their role of offering provision to elderly people and their families, and as a result worked comfortably alongside the private sector. However, if elderly people are to have confidence in social workers and to receive a fair objective professional assessment, then some social workers must re-examine their extreme views that either all private sector homes are exploitative or that they provide a preferred choice every time.

References

1. Townsend, Peter. *The Last Refuge*. Routledge & Kegan Paul, 1962.

2. For example, McCoy, Peter. 'The Data Hare and the Policy Tortoise' *Research, Policy and Planning*. 3, 1, 1985.

3. For example, Johnson, Malcolm. 'Privatising Residential Care: A Review of Changing Policy and Practice'. In Laming, H. (Ed.) *Residential Care for the Elderly*. Policy Studies Institute, London, 1984.

4. For example, Darton, Robin. 'PSSRU Survey of Residential Accommodation for the Elderly 1981: Characteristics of the Residents.' Discussion Paper 426, University of Kent, Canterbury.

5. Kelleher, L. et al. 'Coming to Terms with the Private Sector'. CESSA, 1988.

6. Joseph, Sir Keith, quoted in Booth, Tim. 'Whatever Happened to LAPS?' *Policy and Politics*. 11, 2, 1983, 179.

A Transatlantic View: Privatisation, Canadian-Style

Ernie Lightman, Christa Freiler and John Gandy

Introduction

Privatisation in Canada did not emerge suddenly and cataclysmically, the result of a Thatcher-style revolution in social and political thought. Nor has it always been centre stage, the presumptively best and morally correct way to deliver residual human services, as is the case in the United States. Rather, privatisation Canadian-style has developed in a somewhat ad hoc manner, as much the result of historical accident in particular settings and the federal-provincial dynamic as the outcome of any conscious decision making process.

This chapter contains a brief overview of privatisation within the human services in Canada. It examines the historical framework within which privatisation has developed, touching upon issues of ideology, economics and federal/provincial relations. The recent acceleration in the pace of privatisation is also explored. We then examine two specific areas of concern - the for profit or 'commercial' sector and then the voluntary non-profit fields; the latter encompasses a case example dealing with correctional services. The chapter concludes with some speculative observations about the future of privatisation in Canada in the wake of the 1988 Federal Election and the Free Trade Agreement with the United States.

The context

Any definition of privatisation within the Canadian context must attend to both the voluntary non-profit sector and the commercial or for-profit sector. The former represents the oldest form of human service delivery in the country, with roots that can be traced back to religious activity in the earliest colonial settlements. Hospitals, child welfare, and poverty relief all began in this way and while health care has over the years come to be seen as a governmental responsibility, 'children's aid societies' in Ontario remain to this day as voluntary agencies bearing primary statutory responsibility in the field of child welfare. The Catholic and Jewish communities have even retained their own separate agencies.

Both the non-profit and commercial sectors share a common role in that they respond to social needs that government has failed to acknowledge or treat in an adequate manner; more recently they have both led to, and followed from, decreased government involvement in society. The two also compete directly: in child care, for example, they bid for the limited number of subsidised spaces which a municipality will choose to make available. And, as will be seen below, recent developments predict the accelerated growth of the commercial sector, potentially at the expense of the non-profits.

A major impetus to the growth of privatisation in Canada has occurred since the mid-1970s and, though the rationale may be seen as both ideologically and fiscally based, Wolf[1] has observed that privatisation in Canada 'has been ad hoc and inextricably linked to fiscal restraint'.

Fiscal restraint in turn can only be understood in the context of federal/provincial relations and the division of powers as set out in the British North America Act 1867, and re-affirmed by the Constitution Act 1982. To the provinces go responsibility for most of the human services - health, education, social services, etc. - along with a specific and limited tax base from which to fund these; the federal government by contrast has unlimited access to the tax base but only limited service delivery responsibilities (the correctional example to be considered below represents one of the few areas in which the Federal Government has a direct service delivery function). The result of this constitutional division has been a predictable imbalance at both the federal and provincial levels. Through much of the 1960s and early 1970s Ottawa used its general spending power and budgetary surpluses to entice the provinces and direct their service delivery activities in desired directions. The result was a major expansion in the Canadian welfare state during these years.

Two federal acts are of particular importance. The Canada Assistance Plan (C.A.P.) 1966, is the major piece of federal legislation dealing with social assistance (means tested non-contributory benefits) and allied services. Under the terms of the Act, Ottawa shares with the provinces, on an open-ended basis, fifty per cent of the costs of covered programs, provided certain federal conditions are met. The most relevant of these was a prohibition on the use of for-profit agencies to deliver services.

The Established Programs Financing (E.P.F.) Act 1977 represents lump sum or block funding from Ottawa to the provinces to cover the federal share of costs in the areas of health care (medicare), hospital spending, and post-secondary education. There is no prohibition on for-profit delivery of services. The combined result of these two Acts is that there are today fewer social services delivered on a for-profit basis (C.A.P.) than there are health services (E.P.F.).

Canada was not immune to the onset of monetarism on a world-wide scale in 1975-76. Ottawa became preoccupied with inflation and deficit reduction; the predictable result was a series of attempts to cut back on social spending and to reduce transfer payments to the provinces. A child care bill introduced into the House of Commons just before the 1988 federal election removed this area from the auspices of the Canada Assistance Plan and set an upper limit to federal costs. It also devoted new resources towards subsidising parents, rather than day care places, thereby encouraging parents to 'shop around' among competing sectors in the classic welfare pluralist manner. Federal spending on Established Programs Financing has been cut back in the past several years, not in absolute terms but relative to population growth and to the federal promises at the point of the Act's introduction.[2]

Ottawa's enthusiasm to cut social spending in Canada, unlike Britain, has never been marked by massive widespread cuts or an active dismantling of the welfare state apparatus. Rather, the approach has been gradual, 'an erosion but not a dismantling of social services'.[2] This is in part due to Ottawa's use of what are largely fiscal and financial tools, rather than major direct service responsibilities; it entails the pursuit of what Johnson[2] has described as a 'social services cum economic' strategy. Ottawa simply slows the flow of money to the provinces, and thereby hopes to escape whatever political fallout may emerge.

The assault on social services by Ottawa has thus far been modest. The explanation lies in the co-existence of what Johnson[2] has described as 'two fundamental but antagonistic perspectives of social and economic life in Canada'.

'Bryden speaks of a "market ethos" the cultural expression of the market economy, whose unifying principle was what Macpherson called 'possessive individualism'. But Lipsett and others allude to a general pre-disposition towards state intervention.'[2]

In the social services, this interventionist predisposition has been particularly marked. The free market model has never been as appropriate for dealing with a wide range of social problems.

What Novick[6] has described as 'the welfare state traditions of Europe (alongside) the community populism of North America' has led to a generalised preference for the voluntary non-profit sector, at the expense of the commercial sector, right across Canada, but this may be changing.

In addition to the more common legitimation function, social services in Canada have always served an important accumulation function as well.[3,4] That is, business interests have accepted and indeed desired social services as meeting their own corporate goals and needs. A generalised (almost ideological) hostility towards social service spending on the part of business, which is common in both the U.S. and the U.K., has traditionally been muted in Canada, where the focus has been more pragmatic, for example, concerned with costs and tax levels. This however may be changing in the light of the 1988 federal election.

Canada's Medicare program - publicly funded and universal in coverage - has been seen by business interests as an efficient and effective way to pass to the public treasury (the tax base) as the cost of producing a healthy, and hence a productive, workforce. So, while other services have been subject to the pressures of privatisation, Medicare was actually strengthened against the forces of for-profit delivery through the Canada Health Act 1984; and it is unlikely to come under attack in the near future.[5] Johnson[2] observes that governments in Canada 'have been stridently defensive' of certain programs that have been perceived 'as not interfering with individual initiative'.

This accumulation function for Canada's social services has had two important outcomes in terms of the development of privatisation. First, there has not been the massive replacement of government services by those of the private sector; support for many social services is widespread not only among the public, but historically within parts of the business community as well. Secondly, given this close association between the interests of business and the social services, it has been relatively easy for the commercial sector to enter in and simply take over the for-profit management of certain service areas, when the timing was favourable, i.e. when the Government sought to cut back its own size or expenditures. The process is gradual, perhaps surreptitious and even insidious.

Thus, at the federal level the general approach towards privatisation, followed by both Liberal and Conservative governments since the mid 1970s, has been to leave the form of the welfare state but to slowly starve the content. The provinces for their part have responded to the federal financing squeeze in a variety of ways - off-loading of responsibilities to voluntary non-profit agencies; inaction in the face of new and emerging needs; the use of competitive bidding; contracts; purchase of service, etc.

Though space does not permit detailed examination of the provincial responses, Ismael and Vaillancourt[7] present case studies on privatisation in seven of Canada's ten provinces. They conclude that six of the seven have made 'explicit commitments to the process of privatisation of social service delivery'. Note can certainly be made of British Columbia which has been described as 'Canada's privatisation laboratory'.[8] This province certainly represents Canada's 'most comprehensive and conspicuous privatisation package'[7] in which every available mechanism has been used to reduce government involvement in the economy.

'(The provincial government), like the British Tories, sees privatisation as an end in itself. "Leadership" and "political will" must be used to transfer as much of the public sector as possible to the private one.'[9]

In Alberta the move to privatisation has been defended in terms of 'revitalising community enterprise'[8] and in that province specific privatisation criteria have actually been developed. Ontario, on the other hand, has always relied to a large extent on private, especially non-profit, agencies for the delivery of social services.

With the devolution of state responsibility (and money) come increasing burdens on the voluntary sector, families and communities. The most vivid illustration of this phenomenon is undoubtedly the growth across Canada of 'food banks', another U.S. import, a modern day charitable soup kitchen that so graphically epitomises privatisation of the welfare state.[10]

Commercialisation as a privatisation strategy

The management and delivery of human services by for-profit organisations, or commercialisation, is, as noted earlier, a relatively new form of privatisation in Canada. Historically, the for-profit sector has not played a major role in delivering human services in this country. In fact, the absence of the profit motive was once considered to be one of the distinguishing features of a social welfare system. However, the trend toward privatisation, accompanied by cutbacks in social spending, has created a climate favourable to commercialisation in Canada.

Although not as extensive as in the United States (whence the concept was imported), commercial service provision is now playing a prominent role in service fields previously dominated by the voluntary sector, such as homemaking, children's residences, and day care, as well as replacing government provision of administrative and support services areas, such as corrections and vocational training. Commercialisation is most pronounced, however, in the more profitable health care field. Hospital management, nursing homes, specialised walk-in clinics, and home care are examples of profit initiatives. To illustrate the magnitude of for-profit provision in Canada, at the time of writing about half of the nursing homes for elderly people and half the day care spaces for children in Canada were estimated to be in the hands of for-profit operators. In some provinces, this may be as high as seventy per cent.

The appeal of the for-profit sector

Despite the fact that privatisation has generally been occurring in a haphazard and ad hoc fashion in Canada, some trends are becoming obvious. In a number of provinces, the push to privatisation is manifesting itself in a shift from voluntary to commercial sector delivery.[11] Although some privatisation proponents view any 'private' organisation (either voluntary or for-profit) as preferable to government service delivery, commercialisation is gaining favour with governments at all levels as a privatisation strategy. Advocates of privatisation are arguing that government is not a capable 'doer' in that public enterprise is inherently less productive and less efficient. Private enterprise, especially commercial enterprise, is, on the other hand, considered to be more flexible, innovative, responsive, and cost-conscious. Ironically, it is because of the profit motive, once considered to be incompatible with social welfare provision, that commercial organisations have begun to occupy such a prominent role in many Canadian privatisation proposals. E.C. Manning, a former premier of the province of Alberta, introduced the notion of privatisation to Canada in 1970:

> 'The thing to do is launch a major counter expansion of the private sector into certain fields (social services, in particular) which have erroneously come to be regarded as lying within the jurisdiction of the public sector alone ... Private enterprise must seek to improve the efficiency and quality of essential social services by directly utilising for social action some of the management methods and skills which the competitive pressures of the private sector have developed to a high degree'.[12]

Increasingly popular today is the view that Canada can no longer afford its social welfare system and must turn to the private sector to finance or operate programs:

> 'During the post-war years, Canada built a massive collection of government-run programs that provide us with a first-rate social security net. Today, however, the safety net shows wear and tear at a time when various levels of government can no longer afford the necessary maintenance. Increasingly, they rely on the private sector for more cost-effective services'.[13]

Krashinsky suggests several desirable characteristics of commercial day care centres which he attributes to 'the lure of increased sales and profits', namely: the capacity and willingness of commercial centres to meet increased demand; and their ability to respond to changes in preferences among parents. It should be noted, however, that he also identifies quality control as a major problem in commercial centres.[14]

Notwithstanding the above, there have been no systematic studies in Canada to substantiate the claims of greater efficiency and cost-effectiveness on the part of the commercial sector. The trend to commercialisation has been neither well documented nor well monitored. With the exception of Ontario, there is little information on the scope and consequences of commercialisation in provincial human services.

A 1984 report by the Social Planning Council of Metro Toronto[15] examined the commmmercialisation of health and social services in Ontario and concluded that there were substantial risks associated with increasing the government's reliance on the for-profit sector for the provision of essential human services. The report showed that there was much evidence to support concerns that:

- the profit motive may act as an incentive to cut costs at the expense of service quality, accessibility, and staff salaries;
- accountability to service users and to government is more difficult to ensure with for-profit organizations because of absentee ownership, lack of community involvement, and domination of whole fields of service resulting from corporate concentration; and
- as government increases its reliance on the commercial sector to provide essential service, social policy objectives may be set by organisations whose primary interest is profit.

This last point is increasingly being raised[16]:

'Profit organisations acquire the capacity to organise and supply services on a volume basis. It is when these ventures become the repository of technical knowledge and information, and serve large numbers of people, that control of the market sets in. The risk ... is that the role of government drifts into states of passive intervention, responding to the momentum of profit groups. The regulated begin to set the conditions of their own regulation.'

It is becoming clear that these fears are not unfounded. In Canada as in the United States, the for-profit nursing home and day care 'industries' have organised themselves into powerful lobby groups to delay the implementation of regulatory legislation. The media coverage of the world's first artificial heart transplant in Louisville, Kentucky, in 1984 also highlighted these concerns. According to the Toronto Star newspaper (27/11/84), this situation 'begs the broader issue of who will control the direction of specialised medical care and research in the future.'

Yet, contrary to the claims of the advocates of commercialisation, there is little evidence that the profit motive increases efficiency or makes better use of taxpayers' money. In fact, health care costs are far higher in the U.S. which relies heavily on the commercial sector than they are in Canada.[17,18]

On the positive side, the involvement of the commercial sector has increased the availability of certain services. For-profit organisations also have the financial resources to respond more quickly than may voluntary agencies to government calls for tenders. Some commercial organisations have earned favourable reputations with governments for their flexibility and responsiveness to need. In some cases, however, these apparent advantages have been achieved at the expense of staff salaries and questionable labour practices.[15]

The trend toward increased commercialisation of human services is just beginning to be examined in Canada. Largely as a result of pressure from advocacy organisations and the labour movement, the province of Ontario, Canada's largest and wealthiest province, established a special legislative committee to look into the commercialisation of health and social services in that province. Although the committee never completed its examination because of an intervening provincial election, Ontario has begun to introduce regulatory and legislative provisions expressing a preference for non-profit providers in health care. Whether these intentions will become substantive or merely *pro forma* remains to be seen.

Privatisation of federal correctional services: use of the voluntary non-profit sector

One area in which there is a long history of mixed responsibility between government and voluntary non-profit organisations is the correctional component of the criminal justice system. Although the involvement of the voluntary non-profit sector in corrections began in Canada more than 100 years ago with the establishment of a Prisoner's Aid Association in Toronto, it is only within the last twenty years that there has been an effort to determine the appropriate role for voluntary non-profit organisations and to develop operational policies and procedures. The leadership in this regard has been taken by the federal government because of its responsibility for the administration of the criminal justice system. Policies and practices adopted by Ottawa have been very influential in corrections at the provincial level. Despite the differences in the extent and nature of the use of voluntary non-profit organisations by the relevant provincial ministries, there is a consensus in Canada that government should work closely with voluntary non-profit organisations to provide a variety of programs and services that are at the soft end of corrections and require a minimum of security.[19]

A Task Force on the Role of the Private Sector in Criminal Justice[20] reported in 1977 that there was the need for a partnership of government and voluntary non-profit organisations to ensure a maximum of diversity, choice and citizen participation in the criminal justice system. It recommended that the voluntary non-profit sector have the responsibility for the delivery of a variety of non-custodial correctional services; monitoring government policies, programs and services in the criminal justice sector; and input in policy formulation and the development of standards. The Task Force anticipated that their recommendations would result in greater diversity in the delivery of services; more volunteer involvement in the provision of direct services; and greater dissemination of information and a heightened awareness of citizens about corrections and criminal justice. There is evidence that the Task Force did not regard the involvement of the profit sector as either appropriate or desirable at that time; although it was acknowledged that the voluntary non-profit sector may provide services more cheaply than government, this was not a primary consideration.

However, within a decade, by the 1980s, the 'raison d'etre' for privatisation in corrections and social services was reduction of costs through a smaller number of civil servants and the increase of efficiency and effectiveness through wider use of the voluntary non-profit sector to deliver services. Another change was the federal government decision to explore the use of the commercial sector to deliver services formerly provided through both government and voluntary non-profit organisations.

Neo-conservatives in Canada were attracted by U.S. claims that privatisation of correctional services, and particularly prisons and jails, would make a major contribution to reducing the scope and size of government. Support in the U.S. for privatisation was, and is, based on the 'free market' model, with its emphasis on competition and profit. The alleged, but unsubstantiated, gains of lower costs, greater efficiency, and greater flexibility in correctional services in the U.S. after privatisation did generate some interest among members of Parliament and federal civil servants in Canada.

In general, however, the Canadian federal government provides most of its financial support in corrections through the following types of arrangements: block or lump grants to national voluntary organisations such as the Canadian Criminal Justice Association; unit contracts (e.g., a project to test the effectiveness of a program to assist ex-inmates find employment) and purchase of service contracts (e.g., a per diem rate for residential service). The federal government has not used competitive contracting in its purchase of service contracts with voluntary non-profit organisations. Until very recently these purchase of service contracts covered only eighty per cent of the cost, the balance of which was to be raised in the community through individual contributions or individual grants from the local United Appeal.[21] Thus the community was required to subsidise government correctional programs. The government defended this practice as necessary to ensure that there was meaningful citizen input or participation in Community Based Correctional Programs.

A federal task force that examined the involvement of the private sector, both non-profit and commercial concluded in 1986 that the savings from privatisation will have to come from lower overhead costs, much lower salaries, and limited programmes and staffing. However, the costs of services provided by voluntary non-profit organisations are now approaching or exceeding those of comparable government services. The task force found indications that more supervision and review of voluntary non-profit organisations are necessary, a process which may lead to higher overall costs. In addition they found that some staff in the federal corrections programs believe that the quality of the privately delivered service is poorer and that there is insufficient accountability.[22] No definitive research exists that compares the effectiveness or quality of programs provided by government and not-for-profit organisations.[19,21] Despite the reservations noted above this report concludes that the government should continue to support voluntary non-profit organisations that operate halfway houses, community residential centres and community supervision, if government is willing to provide sufficient funding.

Extensive government support for voluntary non-profit organisations does result in unintended consequences that remain largely unresolved: a reduction in programs and activities by voluntary non-profit agencies in prisoner advocacy and penal reform; the non-profits put in the untenable position of being held responsible for shortcomings or ineffective policies of government in the delivery of services and programs; purchase of service contracts encouraging voluntary non-profit organisations to equate size with success; and a loss of flexibility in programming in voluntary non-profit organisations because government financing is primarily offered to implement its own priorities.[23,24]

In 1987 the federal government decided to experiment with contracts for voluntary non-profit organisations to supervise all parolees in a large metropolitan area. The largest provincial non-profit voluntary organisation in Canada, the John Howard Society of Ontario, re-examined the financing of the voluntary non-profit sector by government and concluded that the ground rules for the partnership were being changed. It recommended that the voluntary non-profit sector should not accept contracts to provide custodial and coercive services (prisons, jails, parole and probation). Not only are these services seen as the preserve of government but the provision of these services by the voluntary non-profit sector will endanger the relationships it has with those who need service. A policy statement reported that the voluntary non-profit sector should limit its contracts from government to those specialised or innovative services that are available to those in the criminal justice system on a voluntary basis.[24]

Another issue that has emerged is the introduction of competitive bidding for contracts. This may result in voluntary non-profit organisations becoming more like their commercial counterparts with an emphasis on costs rather than program.

The future of the partnership of the government and the voluntary non-profit sector in corrections is uncertain. Many believe that if the voluntary non-profit sector continues to resist, or fails to cooperate with, the federal government's moves to contract out direct services, it will look to the commercial sector as has already been the case in some provinces.

Conclusion

Many of the issues raised in this chapter will undoubtedly be familiar to the reader in other countries, as certain underlying dynamics associated with the privatisation process are not nationally bounded. On the other hand, there are issues unique to Canada - the important federal-provincial dimension for example or the rapid introduction of U.S. 'solutions' as a result of the increasing cultural and media fusion between the two countries.

Two other recent developments in Canada will undoubtedly accelerate the pace of privatisation and, in particular, commercialisation. The first of these, the 'Meech Lake Accord', represents the final step in repatriating the Canadian Constitution and envisages a more decentralised federal state than is the case today. Though final passage of the Accord is as yet uncertain, if approved, it will clearly facilitate the provinces' pursuit of various privatised options.

The other issue, the Conservative victory in the November 1988 federal election, approved free trade with the United States. Through a generalised increased American presence in Canada, the residual market-based values of that society are certain to follow. The Treaty itself permits the 'unfettered entry'[25] of American firms into the management of a wide range of health and social services - 31 specific areas are enumerated. In addition, there are pressures to place commercial and non-profit suppliers of services on an equal footing, so that a Canadian government could not give preferential treatment to a community-based, non-profit day care centre over a U.S.-based multinational. The threat to the social services from the Free Trade Agreement is massive and potentially catastrophic, and privatisation is only one part of this looming disaster.

References

1. Wolf, J. 'Can Voluntary Nonprofits Survive Privatization? Changing the Social Contract' *Business Quarterly*. November, 1986, 62-69.

2. Johnson, A. F. 'Federal Policies and the Privatization of Provincial Social Services'. In Ismael, J. and Vaillancourt, Y. (Eds.) *Privatization and Provincial Social Services in Canada*. University of Alberta Press, Edmonton, 1988.

3. O'Connor, J. *Fiscal Crisis of the State*. St. Martin's Press, New York, 1973.

4. Buchbinder, H. 'Inequality and the Social Services'. In Moscovitch, A. and Drover, G. (Eds.) *Inequality*. University of Toronto Press, Toronto, 1981.

5. Tsalikis, G. 'Canada's Health Services'. In Drover, G. (Ed.) *Free Trade and Social Policy*. Canadian Council on Social Development, Ottawa, 1988, 103-124.

6. Novick, M. 'The Future of Voluntarism'. In *A New Era for Voluntarism*, Proceedings of a Conference held in Toronto, June 1-3, 1986, United Way of Greater Toronto, Toronto, 1986.

7. Ismael, J. and Vaillancourt, Y. *Privatization and Provincial Social Services in Canada*. University of Alberta Press, Edmonton, 1988.

8. Freiler, C. 'Privatization and Commercialization'. In *A New Era for Voluntarism*, Proceedings of a Conference held in Toronto, June 1-3, 1986, United Way of Greater Toronto, Toronto, 1986.

9. Scott, I. 'Privatization'. In *Three Deals: One Game*. Women's Economic Agenda, Vancouver, 1988.

10. Riches, G. *Beyond the Safety Net: Food Banks in Canada*. Canadian Council on Social Development, Ottawa, 1987.

11. Hurl, L. and Freiler, C. 'Privatized Human Services: The Ontario Experience'. Paper presented at the Second Conference on Provincial Social Welfare Policy, Calgary, May 1-3, 1985.

12. M. & M. Systems Research Limited. *Requests for Proposals and Social Contracts, a Strategy to Advance the Role of Private Enterprise in Canada*. Edmonton, 1970, 3.

13. Zeidenberg, J. 'Privatizing the Welfare State'. *Small Business*. October 1988, 42.

14. Krashinsky, M. *Day Care and Public Policy in Ontario*. Ontario Economic Council, Toronto, 1977.

15. Freiler, C. *Caring for Profit: The Commercialization of Human Services in Ontario*. Social Planning Council of Metro Toronto, Toronto, 1984.

16. Novick, M. 'Social Policy and the Search for a Provincial Framework'. In MacDonald, D. (Ed.) *The Government and Policies of Ontario*. Van Nostrand Reinhold, Ltd., Toronto, 1980.

17. Weller, G. and Manga, P. 'The Push for Reprivatization of Health Care Services in Canada, Britain and the United States' *Journal of Health Politics, Policy and Law*. 8, 3, Fall 1988, 500.

18. Ontario Federation of Labour. 'What Private Control of Health Care Means'. In *Ontario Labour*, Toronto, 1985.

19. Ericson, R. V., McMahon, M. S. and Evans, D. G. 'Punishing For Profit: Reflections on the Revival of Privatization In Corrections' *Canadian Journal of Criminology*. 29, 4, 1987, 355-388.

20. Canada, Ministry of the Solicitor General of Canada. *Report of the Task Force on the Role of the Private Sector in Criminal Justice*, Vol. II. Ottawa: Ministry of Supply and Services Canada, 1977.

21. Gandy, J. *Privatization of Correctional Services for Adults*. Solicitor General of Canada, Ottawa, 1985.

22. Canada, *The Justice System - A Study Team Report to the Task Force on Program Review. (The Nelson Report)*. Ministry of Supply and Services Canada, 1986.

23. Gandy, J. 'Costs and Benefits to the Voluntary Sector: Privatization in Corrections' *The John Howard Society of Ontario Newsletter*. Winter/Spring, 1984.

24. John Howard Society of Ontario. *Privatization and Commercialization of Correctional Services*. Draft manuscript, June 1986.

25. Orr, J. *The Free Trade Agreement and Social Policy: A Policy Paper*. Social Planning Council of Metro Toronto, Toronto, 1988.

Privatising Prison Services

Stephen Shaw

In May 1988 the Home Office took over the Alma Dettingen military barracks near Camberley in Surrey as a temporary overflow prison. This was part of an emergency government package endeavouring (unsuccessfully, as it turned out) to clear police cells in London of remand prisoners for whom no room could be found in the gaols. With its echoes of the Crimean War (the river Alma was forced by the Anglo-French army on 20 September 1854) and now staffed by military police and guarded by troops of the Gurkha Regiment, the use of Alma Dettingen seemed to symbolise the failure of over a century of state control of the prisons.

This is particularly the case because the aspect of Alma Dettingen which excited most interest in the Home Office was that the catering contract to provide food for the 300 prisoners had been privatised. For this - the employment of a few service wives by a small catering company - was virtually the first breach of the State monopoly of incarceration since 1878 when Parliament passed a Prison Act which brought the county gaols and recidivist prisons under the control of central government. Indeed, the prison service has a reasonable claim to be Britain's first and most enduring nationalised industry. Accordingly, and given the unique place of law and order amongst the responsibilities of government, any privatisation within the prisons is of peculiar historical significance.

Defining privatisation

As with other state industries, the use of the term privatisation in the context of the prison service encompasses a variety of options. It could of course - as with British Gas or British Telecom - involve the wholesale transfer of assets from the public to the private sector. It could imply lease-back or buy-back arrangements whereby the ownership of the assets rests in the private sector while management remains a public responsibility. (This would not entirely be an innovation. Oxford Prison is an ancient monument owned by the City Council and leased to the Home Office. Dartmoor Prison and its extensive estate is owned by Prince Charles through the Duchy of Cornwall). It could mean the sub-contracting of particular services - for example, escort duties between prison and court, the running of prison workshops or the laundry or, as we have seen, of catering. Or it could involve private construction, ownership and management of certain classes of institution complementing - or, in some circumstances, competing against - the state sector.

Before considering some of these options in more detail, it is worth tracing the development of recent interest in Britain in privatisation and the penal system. It is after all only a few short years ago that the very notion of privatising prisons would have been regarded as an absurdity. There is no text book on penal policy yet in print which even mentions the possibility. Law and order - no less than national defence - was regarded on all sides, almost by definition, as a necessarily direct responsibility of the State. Indeed, it remains the case today on the Conservative benches in the House of Commons that even otherwise vociferous supporters of the government's privatisation programme have publicly drawn the line at the prisons.

In fact, this argument ignores the fact that over the past twenty five years the role of the police in many respects has been taken over by private security companies. The escorting of wage rolls and the growth and number of store detectives are examples. And the provision of many non-custodial options for young offenders has been subcontracted to voluntary (albeit non-profit making) agencies. It has been argued forcefully, and perhaps surprisingly, by two socialist criminologists, Ryan and Ward,[1] that the State has a proper monopoly of the *allocation* of punishment but not necessarily of its *delivery*.

Notwithstanding the flawed logic which lay behind the casual acceptance of the State monopoly of corrections, it was not until 1984 that the right-wing think-tank, the Adam Smith Institute[2] first proposed privatisation of penal services in Britain as part of a general critique of the criminal justice system as a whole. Press reports also indicated support from one Conservative MP (Michael Forsyth, currently a junior minister in the Scottish Office).

The argument of the Adam Smith Institute was that political interference with the prison service prevented the necessary capital investment and managerial flexibility and innovation:

> 'It is surprising that the idea of independently built and managed prisons has not had a wider audience in Britain nor gained acceptance. Both security firms and hotel operations are commonplace in the private sector: it may be an over-simplification but a prison, borstal [sic], or detention centre involves little more than a combination of these two talents'(p.64).

Subsequently, the Institute published a book by Peter Young[3] which pointed to the 'producer dominance' (i.e. Prison Officers' Association influence) upon prisons policy and presented a roseate view of the American experience with privatisation:

'Perhaps the most surprising facts... are the greatly improved conditions for prisoners in all the US private jails. These improved conditions have been hailed by the prisoners themselves and by disinterested observers such as local media and clergy. That costs can be cut is not very surprising... but that private firms can both cut costs and improve standards is certainly worth noting. Perhaps the most compelling argument for prison privatisation is therefore the humanitarian one' (p.38).

Young's book is presently the most comprehensive review of American developments which has been published in Britain. However, the bases of his conclusions - US press reports and information provided by the private companies themselves - can scarcely be regarded as the most rigorous or the most objective.

Support was also to come from criminologists sympathetic to the penal reform lobby. For example, the *Independent* newspaper reported Dr. Ken Pease and Professor Maxwell Taylor[4] as favouring wholesale denationalisation with private institutions competing with each other for contracts on the basis of their success in achieving the rehabilitation of prisoners. And Sean McConville and Eryl Hall Williams argued:

'The private sector should be more involved than at present in the provision of services to prisoners and persons accused of crime. In particular, we see the following areas as being suitable for the introduction of some private enterprise involvement:

1) Work for prisoners under contract for outside employers.

2) Contracting out certain prison services

    A) Kitchens and catering

    B) Half-way houses

    C) Certain detention services, possibly excluding high-security prisoners

    D) Leasing premises

    E) Medical services

    F) Court and escort service.'

However, the real pressure for privatisation did not take off until publication in May 1987 of a House of Commons Home Affairs Select Committee report consisting of just three pages and entitled *Contract Provision of Prisons*.[6] Following a short visit to the United States, the Committee recommended (the Labour Members dissenting):

'... that the Home Office should, as an experiment, enable private sector companies to tender for the construction and management of custodial institutions. Such contracts should contain standards and requirements and failure to meet them would be grounds for the Government's terminating a contract. The standards should be made legally enforceable against contractors. We also recommend that tenders should be invited in particular for the construction and management of new remand centres, because it is there that the worst overcrowding in the prison system is concentrated.'

It is an intriguing commentary on the making of public policy that it was the personal interest in the idea of privatised prisons of just two Conservative backbenchers on the Home Affairs Committee which placed the issue so firmly on the political agenda. They were Sir Edward Gardner - who retired from the Commons at the 1987 General Election and who, controversially, now chairs one of the private consortia angling for prison contracts - and John Wheeler, a former Borstal assistant governor and Home Office civil servant. Both were distinguished Parliamentarians who enjoyed the respect of their colleagues. Parenthetically, it may also be noted Gardner and Wheeler are well known for their general sympathies for the penal reform lobby - indeed, John Wheeler is currently chairman of the influential Parliamentary All-Party Penal Affairs Group, one of the most active and effective all-party groupings at Westminster.

Following the Select Committee's report, support for the idea of privatised remand facilities was to come almost immediately from the Chairman of the Parole Board and Conservative peer, Lord Windlesham.[7] Furthermore, in his brilliant and unjustly neglected analysis of the 1986 prison riots in England, HM Chief Inspector of Prisons[8] suggested that court escort duties - which in England and Wales are carried out by prison officers - could be a plum target for privatisation.

The commercial interests were also quick off the mark and a consortium was formed by two of the biggest construction companies, Mowlem and McAlpine, plus the 'market leader' in private prisons in the United States, the Corrections Corporation of America (CCA). Meanwhile, the Prisons Minister, the Earl of Caithness, was sent to America to investigate private prisons along with that other US innovation attracting support from within the British Conservative Party - the electronic tagging of offenders.

What Caithness discovered was that the American experience of privatisation was extremely limited and had been relentlessly hyped by the companies involved. Less than 0.5 per cent of America's admittedly high number of prisoners were detained in a private prison. There is no private gaol at the Federal level. At the time of his visit, neither was there a private prison at State level (there are now two or three open prisons in Oklahoma, Kentucky and Tennessee).Only at the lowest level of the American tripartite system - the county jails - were any private institutions to be found, (about twenty in all). In other words, even CCA (which, incidentally, is a subsidiary of the Kentucky Fried Chicken conglomerate) is responsible for only a dozen or so facilities, all of them with minimum security. The prisons-for-profit industry is 'still in its embryonic stage', with few companies past 'the start-up phase'.[9]

It is true that a number of the Immigration Detention Centres along the Rio Grande are also in private hands but Caithness did not have to cross the Atlantic to find similar privatised arrangements. The Immigration Detention Centre at Harmondsworth on the edge of Heathrow Airport is run by Securicor, the contract having been agreed by the last Labour Government (reportedly to keep it out of the hands of the Prison Officers' Association). The smaller facility at Gatwick known as the Beehive and - until it ran aground - the redundant ferry tied up at Harwich on the East Coast and used for Tamil refugees were also managed under contract to the Home Office by Securicor.

It is also true that the sub-contracting of prison services occurs in some institutions in the majority of individual states in the US. Lease-back arrangements are also becoming more popular with prison administrators as they avoid the necessity for prior legislative and electoral approval for new construction. However, in general, the large Wall Street corporations have held back (although this may change now that CCA is forecasting profitability for its enterprises). Moreover, it seems that most corporate interest is in construction, not in management contracts.

Incidentally, although the rest of the world lacks privately run prisons, apparently one US firm is prospecting in Latin America and there is reputedly a single private institution in Panama. The French Conservative government of 1986-8 considered but rejected private prisons although consortia including CCA are building new gaols and will be running sub-contracted services.

Government policy

What then does the British Government have in mind? Evidence is now emerging of a major shift in the government's position over the winter of 1987/88.

The private management of institutions seemed at first to have been wholly rejected by the government. In January 1987, the then Permanent Secretary at the Home Office, Sir Brian Cubbon, told the House of Commons Expenditure Committee that no work was being undertaken into privatisation. Later in the year, in July, when challenged on the same point, Home Secretary Douglas Hurd[10] was remarkably forthright:

'I do not think there is a case, and I do not believe that the House would accept a case, for auctioning or privatising the prisons or handing over the business of keeping prisoners safe to anyone other than government servants. However, I do not think that we can afford to sit back and say that the way in which we have been doing things in the prison building programme is absolute and cannot be improved.'

However, when Lord Caithness[11] addressed the Annual Conference of Boards of Visitors (the equivalent of Visiting Committees in Scotland) in September 1987, a new element had been introduced:

'The first point to make is that the government has no intention of selling off prisons to be run as a completely separate enterprise from government. To do so would represent a complete abdication of one of our most important responsibilities, that of ensuring that custodial sentences imposed by the courts are given proper effect. At the same time, we believe that it is seriously worth considering whether the private sector may not be able to help us run the service more efficiently and effectively than at present. There are two main areas for private sector involvement to which we are giving particular attention: the provision of new accommodation and the possibility that the private sector might be invited to tender for the operation and management of a new facility, perhaps for remand prisoners under contract.'

In other words, a distinction was being made between private institutions for convicted prisoners and those for unconvicted prisoners.

Principally, of course, what the government was talking about was ways of accelerating the (pound)one billion prison building programme. However, there was less to this than meets the eye. Some eighty per cent of prison building costs are already 'privatised' (architects' and lawyers' fees, construction costs) and prisoners were no longer a ʳʳed to build their own prison as they had been from the time when Dartmoor was built by Napoleonic prisoners of war right up to a decade ago. Rather, the Home Office is known to be dissatisfied with the Property Services Agency, the government department which oversees building contracts of new prisons (the Home Office itself oversees the renovation and extension of existing gaols). A succession of building scandals - poor workmanship, delays and cost over-runs (catalogued by the National Audit Office[12]) - had already led to the establishment of a Prison Building Board within the Home Office which included three private sector representatives. However, the much-vaunted 'private sector techniques' did not seem on the face of it to amount to more than the less-than-revolutionary policy of replicating the same design on a number of different sites.

Indeed, although there were reports that catering, laundry, clothing and maintenance contracts might be put out to tender, it was said that the provisions of the 1952 Prison Act prevented the Home Secretary from sub-contracting whole institutions to the private sector. Added to the known disquiet among senior prison governors about the difficulties of enforcing control in all-remand institutions, and the repeated delay in responding formally to the Home Affairs Committee report, it looked as if privatisation had not even reached first base. As a threat, it was a useful stick to beat the PDA - which was fighting the implementation of the 'Fresh Start' package on wages and working practices (in Scotland, a similar package to 'Fresh Start' is known as the Grand Design). However, as a policy it frankly did not appear to be a runner.

However, by March 1988 all of this had changed. A letter from the Home Office was posted to some forty companies and consortia which had expressed an interest, inviting them to submit detailed proposals for the construction of new open prisons and remand centres. At the same time, heavy hints were dropped that management contracts were in the offing. In particular, it appeared that a decision in principle had been taken in favour of privately-run remand facilities where management is at least not involved in such quasi-judicial functions as parole decision-making and the loss of remission for breaches of prison discipline. A Green Paper on all aspects of the remand system (including escort duties and the provision of secure and semi-secure accommodation) was promised for before the Summer Recess.

What appears to have happened over the winter of 1987-88 is that the continuing mismatch between the number of prisoners and the number of prison places, combined with growing concern on the part of the Treasury regarding escalating costs of the prison building programme, led the government to seek quicker and cheaper building methods and to investigate the possibility of the requisite capital being raised through the commercial market. However, Ministers were also reflecting a change of mood on the part of senior civil servants and some prison governors. Initially highly suspicious of privatisation, it was becoming increasingly clear that they were taking the view that private prisons could hardly be worse-run than the ones for which the State had had responsibility for more than a century.

Thus when the promised Green Paper was published in July 1988[13] it was no surprise that the government, while admitting practical problems, could argue that it was:

> 'not at present inclined to accept that there is any over-riding difficulty of private sector involvement, providing that sensible practical safeguards are built into the arrangements.'

Three specific proposals were put forward. Firstly, it was argued that 'more secure' bail hostels with 'a more structured daytime programme' could be provided by the private sector - an indication that privatisation would enter the province of the probation service as well as the prisons. (Another Home Office Green Paper, *Punishment, Custody and the Community*[14] also discussed the possibility 'for the probation service to contract with other services, and private and voluntary organisations, to obtain some of the components of punishment in the community'). Secondly, it was suggested that the escort and court duties of prison staff would in most instances be taken over by private contractors. The third proposal was that new remand centres would be built *and* managed by the private sector. Simple arithmetic suggests that if only one of these private remand centres gets the go-ahead, Britain will immediately take the lead over the United States in the proportion of its prisoners held in private gaols.

The case for and against

The practical problems that will result from privatisation are substantial. From where will a private contractor recruit its staff? How will they be trained? Will the private sector cream off low security prisoners leaving the State to deal with those who present a high risk? How will contracts be enforced given that, unlike say the contract provision of local authority cleaning or rubbish collecting services, there will scarcely be a large number of other firms with the trained staff and management expertise to take over contracts at short notice?

However, no less intriguing than the specific plans of the government as they appear at the moment, are the theoretical dangers *and* benefits of privatising prison services. In some quarters, of course, to talk of the potential benefits of privatisation is tantamount to heresy. Certainly the penal reform movement, having first kept its head down and hoping the issue would go away, has been vehemently critical of private sector involvement. The privately-managed penal hell-holes of the Eighteenth Century have been presented as the likely model for privatisation 200 years later. Evidence produced by the Prison Officers' Association for the Home Affairs Select Committee has been repeated uncritically. Evidence of 'scruffy and thug-like warders' and the POA claim that 'we have never witnessed such shocking conditions' have been quoted by people who would normally treat what the POA say with extreme caution.

In fact, the penal reform lobby in the United States is unable to provide much support for the view that American private prisons are poorly run, with barren regimes, decrepit conditions, and sadistic guards. The present writer has found that efforts to dig up the dirt have been unavailing.[15] Indeed, one or two of the US private prisons appear to be model institutions (perhaps not surprisingly if the American companies regard themselves as being, in the words of one enthusiast, 'at the cutting edge of a whole new industry'). There is currently no reason to believe that the best private prisons are superior to the best Federal or State prisons. Equally, there is no convincing proof that the worst privately-run institutions are inferior to the large number of appalling county gaols to be found in the southern states.

What then are the possible advantages of private sector involvement with the prisons? The first argument is quite simply the mess which the State has made of running the prisons for the last 100 years. Conditions and regimes are poor while costs (especially security costs) have escalated. There is surely something to be said for the view that this was only to be expected of any monopoly, insulated from competitive pressures and lacking a convincing consumer lobby. The prison service has become unresponsive and bureaucratic, charging the taxpayer a higher price for a lower level of output (and in the grip of trade union power) than would occur under competitive conditions. To put it more plainly, are we really saying to prisoners in Wandsworth, Durham or Barlinnie that their conditions would be worse if they were in private hands?

The second argument for at least some degree of private sector involvement derives from the case for 'normalising' the prison environment, breaking down the status of prisons as 'cultural as well as physical enclaves'.[16] Here, for example, are two of our best known academic observers of penal policy, Rod Morgan and Roy King[17]:

'services within the prison should be provided by the same commercial, voluntary or statutory agencies which normally provide them within the community.'

It is true that 'normalisation' usually refers to medical, welfare and chaplaincy services but there is no reason in principle why it should not apply equally to prison workshops, prison catering and so on. It is indeed difficult to see the objection if we wish to see similar standards applying in prison as outside and if we wish to break down the prison as a total institution. On the other hand, few private companies are likely to be very interested in providing the services which matter most to prisoners such as the prison canteen or prison shop. In other words, the practical results - like those flowing from civilianisation in the police and the prisons - are likely to be disappointingly marginal.

Perhaps the most peculiar argument of all for privatisation is that of accountability since the very lack of accountability and fear of unchecked abuse is one of the most common criticisms of private prisons. Yet in some circumstances a private prison could be *more* rather than less accountable. By definition any sub-contracting involves a *contract* between the State and the private company, the terms of which represent in essence a set of minimum standards, breach of which would render the contract void. This is of course a very different situation from the state-run prisons in England and Scotland which frequently breach their own rules with impunity, the courts taking the view that the Prison Rules are non-judicial. As the government admits in its Green Paper, 'contracts will have to set clear and enforceable standards', adding 'in the present prison system there is no existing document which lays out comprehensively and in detail the requirements for a remand centre regime. One will therefore have to be developed for this purpose.' In other words, privatisation necessarily implies setting standards.

What matters in practice is whether breaches of contract would actually be penalised. We have already noted the difficulty of finding an alternative private contractor at short notice and certainly one of the consortia angling for prison contracts in England has openly stated that it would take no notice of government-imposed standards[18]: 'We would do what we can to make a prison cheaper, so long as the specification was left entirely to us.' However, if (and it is a big 'if') standards could be agreed which were tough, verifiable, and strictly enforced, then private prisons could be more publicly accountable for their regimes and conditions than the publicly managed prisons themselves. Since that plainly would be unsatisfactory, there is a case for saying that privatisation would inevitably lead to the establishment of a code of minimum standards for all our prisons.

These possible advantages of privatisation are not negligible. However, there are powerful arguments of both principle and practice in the opposite direction. Leaving aside the questionable ethics of deriving private profit from incarceration, the creation of a powerful commercial lobby with a vested interest in an expanding prison population runs the danger of subverting the making of penal policy. In addition, it would be totally unacceptable for private concerns to be involved in such functions as prison discipline and parole which directly determine the effective length of a prison sentence. Nor is there any guarantee of continual public and Parliamentary accountability (MPs' questions about Harmondsworth Detention Centre, for example, were dodged for many years by both Labour and Conservative Ministers on the ground of 'commercial confidentiality').

At the same time, there is as yet no convincing evidence that privatised prisons are actually cheaper. Harmondsworth, for example, is considerably more expensive than an equivalent prison. For private jails to become a cheaper option, there is an obvious danger that financial considerations will take precedence - even more than they do at present - over questions of humane regimes, decent standards, and staff safety, training and welfare. In other words, prisons might be run with a maximum of technology (which is relatively cheap) and a minimum of human contact (which is relatively expensive). Equally, even if we assume that the competitive tendering for prison services results in the cheapest option, is it to be the best option for prisoners? Who is the consumer of prison services: the prisoners or the state? Privatisation is not a market solution for prisoners. Nobody is suggesting that they will have a choice of public or private accommodation.

In our present state of knowledge - with little empirical evidence to go on - the possible advantages and dangers of prison privatisation seem to this writer to be more closely balanced than many critics have allowed. We should be sceptical of the claim that private affluence will necessarily replace or mitigate public squalor. The history of privatised services is after all a shoddy one with poor services replacing more expensive ones. But we should be no less sceptical of the proposition that *only* the state can be responsible for the delivery of punishment - not because it does it well but because the alternative is to revert to the penal practices of two centuries ago. There are of course real questions of public accountability and the enforcement of standards. Moreover, given the particular stresses upon remand prisoners (which manifest themselves in higher than average rates of disciplinary offences, self-mutilation and suicide), there must be genuine concern about the calibre and number of staff which a private contractor would employ. However, the limited American experience suggests that the fundamental critique of privatisation should rest on its expansionist potential (are more prisons a useful social investment?) rather than on comparisons with the Eighteenth Century.

Privatised prisons seem on the face of it to be so inherently unlikely to be introduced that it is difficult to take the idea seriously. Yet it is likely that within the next five years the private sector will be responsible for at least some proportion of the prison system in England and Wales. In a related development, there is also growing talk of the prison service enjoying 'agency status' along the lines proposed generally for the public sector by Sir Robin Ibbs and as it did until 1961 under the Prison Commission.[19]

If the argument of principle is not sufficient to prevent the privatising of custody, it must equally be expected that the privatising of some aspects of the non-custodial sector will not be far behind. Although there has been less public debate on the issue, the management of hostels, community service schemes, day centres, even electronic monitoring or 'tagging' could all potentially be provided on a contract basis, whether by profit-making firms or by not-for-profit companies established by the voluntary sector. Clearly, there would be practical considerations analogous to those for private prisons: staff qualifications and training, the quality of the service provided, standards and the enforcement conditions in contracts. No less significantly, there would be the worry that a two-tier system would be created, discriminating against less 'attractive' offender-clients: people with drink, drug or mental health problems, for example. It is also uncertain how sub-contracting particular classes of penalty would be consistent with the statutory duties of probation officers and social workers in enforcing the orders of the court. All of these factors present major difficulties. However, in the context of the non-custodial sector, at least the expansionist tendencies of private contractors would be operating in the direction of a reduction in this country's excessive use of imprisonment.

References

1. Ryan, M. and Ward, T. 'Prisons, Privatisation and the Role of the State'. In Matthews, R. (Ed.) *The Privatisation of Criminal Justice*. Forthcoming.

2. Adam Smith Institute. *Omega Justice Policy*. ASI (Research) Ltd, London, 1984.

3. Young, P. *The Prison Cell*. ASI (Research) Ltd, London, 1987.

4. The *Independent*. 5 March 1987.

5. McConville, S. and Hall Williams, E. *Crime and Punishment: A Radical Rethink*. Tawney Society, London, 1985.

6. Fourth Report from the Home Affairs Committee, *Contract Privision of Prisons*. HC Paper 291, 1987.

7. *The Times*. July 8 1987.

8. Home Office. *Report of an Inquiry by HM Chief Inspector of Prisons into the Disturbances in Prison Service Establishments in England between 29 April - 2 May 1986*. HC Paper 42, 1987.

9. Borna, S. 'Free Enterprise goes to Prison' *British Journal of Crimonology*. October, 1986.

10. House of Commons Debates, 16 July 1987, col. 1299.

11. Speech released by Home Office Press Office.

12. National Audit Office. *Home Office and Property Services Agency: Programme for the Provision of Prison Places*. HC Paper 135, 1985.

13. *Private Sector Involvement in the Remand System*. CM 434, 1988.

14. *Punishment, Custody and the Community*. Cm 424, 1988.

15. Shaw, S. 'Privatisation and Penal Reform' *Prison Report: the Quarterly Newsletter of the Prison Reform Trust*. November, 1987.

16. Morgan, R. and King, R. 'Profiting from Prison' *New Society*. 23 October 1987.

17. King, R.D. and Morgan, R. *The Future of the Prison System*. Gower, Farnborough, 1980.

18. *The Independent*. November 18 1987.

19. *The Times*. August 4 1988.